Little Voice Mastery™

Little Voice Mastery™

How to Win the War

Between Your Ears

in 30 Seconds or Less and

Have an Extraordinary Life!

Second Edition

BLAIR SINGER

SelectBooks, Inc.
New York

This edition published by SelectBooks, Inc.
For information address SelectBooks, Inc., New York, New York.

Second Edition

ISBN 978-1-59079-215-5

Cataloging-in-Publication Data

Singer, Blair.
  Little voice mastery : how to win the war between your ears in 30 seconds or less and have an extraordinary life! / Blair Singer. -- 2nd ed.
       p. cm.
  Summary: "CEO of leading company providing sales training and personal growth coaching describes surprisingly easy-to-master techniques to empower people to go beyond their ordinary selves to achieve peak performance"--Provided by publisher.
  ISBN 978-1-59079-215-5 (pbk. : alk. paper)
  1. Success--Psychological aspects. 2. Self-confidence. 3. Self-esteem.
  4. Self-realization. I. Title.
  BF637.S8S5456 2011
  158.1--dc22
                          2011006868

Manufactured in the United States of America
10 9 8 7 6 5 4 3 2

Dedications

Little Voice Mastery is dedicated to the hundreds of thousands of incredible souls who have weathered through my programs, seminars, tele-seminars, e-mails, articles, and books. Those folks who were put into large and small rooms by their bosses in Fortune 50 companies and Mom and Pop shops down the block. My friends, my family, my siblings, my business partners all seem to have been sent here to teach me something about who I am supposed to be. They have loved me, nurtured me, scolded me, challenged me, and even opposed me ... but at every juncture have taught me.

This book is dedicated to my two boys, Ben and Zachary. Teaching them to manage the "little voice" will give them the lives they deserve. They have taught me more about life, presence, and energy management than anything I have done in my life.

Everyone at some point in their life has a dream or a vision of who they could be. As we grow, sometimes that vision gets battered, minimized, or even obscured. This book is dedicated to that vision of who you are supposed to be. That is the real you. It has always been there. Having a glimpse of that vision is like a lick of ice cream, and as Bucky Fuller said, "You wouldn't be given a lick of the ice cream unless you were meant to have the whole cone!" So I'll say it again: This book is dedicated to you. The real you.

Before you turn another page…

Go to
www.littlevoicemastery.com/diagnostic
right now!

Take your FREE "Little Voice" Assessment
to find out
where your "Little Voice" is helping you—
or shooting you in the foot!

**You'll do it again at the end of the book
to see your growth just from reading!**

Contents

Preface

Greetings. My name is Blair Singer.

We may have met through one of my two Rich Dad's Advisors books, *SalesDogs* or *The ABC's of Building a Business Team That Wins*. Or we may have met at one of the thousands of corporate trainings, public seminars or keynote speeches I have delivered over the past twenty-seven years.

As a trainer, teacher, coach, and business owner, I have worked with hundreds of thousands of people helping them to achieve higher levels of income, satisfaction, performance, and growth. The same is true for thousands of businesses around the world.

Through all of these interactions there has been one secret weapon that has been the difference for every successful individual in every case. It is the knowledge and application of Little Voice Mastery which you are about to discover. It is what gives you your dreams—or blocks them.

Stay tuned. This book is in two parts. The first part will reveal to you what your Little Voice REALLY is and how to master it so that you can have an extraordinary life.

The second part is 21 actual techniques that you can apply in less than 30 seconds to shift your point of view, control your emotions or simply master the Little Voice that battles for control of your being. It is quite okay to simply jump to Part Two to get right to the techniques. Or take them in order. Either way, you will notice positive thoughts, actions and changes immediately.

If this book is our first introduction to each other, I am honored. If we have met before, it's great to speak to you again. Let's get started!

Acknowledgments

While most people tend to skip the acknowledgment section of a book in order to get onto the main topic at hand ... to me, particularly as an author, it is one of the most important parts of the book. It's important because any piece of work such as a book, a piece of art, a business, a relationship, a career, or even a family is really a "body of work." By that I mean this book, like all of the other artifacts I mentioned above, is simply an embodiment of other great minds, intense experiences, incredible teaching and mentoring, as well as incredible sacrifices and learnings on the part of many who have come before me.

Nothing in this book is original. As a matter of fact, if I hear one more person quote Anthony Robbins, Napoleon Hill, or Socrates and claim it to be their own or without acknowledging where it came from ... I will personally choke them. The true sign of leadership is the willingness to acknowledge and honor source. Done with honor and humility, you then can truly call it your own.

Anything that I have been able to accomplish today has been a direct result of what others have taught me, challenged me to do, supported me through, coached me and even taunted me to accomplish.

I have been waging the battle between my ears my entire life. I actually love it!!! When I win that battle, I grow, my relationships get better, my health gets better, and my income soars. The size of my game expands. When I lose ... I learn. So you see, there is no way that I can really lose. R. Buckminster Fuller taught me that; even though I never met him, I have studied him intently and feel like he is always whispering in at least one of my ears.

The incredible coaching, teaching, and clearing from Alan Walter has been instrumental in allowing me to clear my brain to the degree that I am able to deal with more complexity without the stress and get on to be who I need to be. Jayne Johnson has not only been a friend for many years, but also a great "clearing practitioner" who has imparted some of the most awesome communication skills I know. She has been the person I go to when my "little voice" is beating me up. Both of these folks have had tremendous input directly and indirectly to this series.

My dear friend Robert Kiyosaki, who is probably the only living person who is as relentless about going after his "little voice" as I am, has not only been a great friend and partner all these years, but the source of continual challenge to me to be the best that I can be. He has taught me strength, 100 percent responsibility, and how to find humor and resourcefulness in even the toughest of times. He continues to push me to bigger games. To his wife Kim, who has always supported, nurtured, and challenged me—not only as a business partner, but as a friend who continues to give the gift of radiance, optimism, and joy.

To Kelly Ritchie, who is not only my best friend, but business partner in one of the biggest business games on earth. Over these many years, he has taught me trust, perseverance, and vision. These are gifts that no one could ever ask for.

Besides putting me in the best physical shape of my life, Mack Newton has had an extraordinary contribution to this body of work. His relentless coaching, his understanding of what creates peak performance and his processes of getting the most out of just about anybody has changed my life and the lives of thousands. He has shown me that there is a new gear in my life and has taught me how to find and tap the farthest reaches of my mind to get to it.

I also want to thank Kim White, formerly a world-class distance runner and crazy Australian, whose gift of being able to see the un-seeable and clear physical, mental, spiritual, and emotional space is now world renown.

I want to thank Marshal Thurber whose brilliance in teaching and personal development got me started on working on me. He taught me well. To Lawrence West, Carol Lacey, and others who prefer to remain nameless who were some of my best "little voice" teachers. To Danny Gayle, Randolph Craft, and the Honolulu team that kicked me out of the world of unconsciousness and onto this path of working on me.

To my partner Marco Antonio Regil, who is not only a great spokesperson for the "little voice," but a great friend and mentor who continually forces me to "up my game." His commitment to deliver this message to the Spanish-speaking world will change the lives of millions.

To our selfless team and our incredible SalesPartner™ franchisees all over the world, who put their hearts on the line for a mission bigger than they know. To Richard and Veronica Tan, who change the lives of millions in Asia, Mona Gambetta who made this book a reality, and hundreds of others who have put themselves on stage with me, responded to emails, sat in hot seats, and took what they learned and converted it to incredible financial, spiritual, and emotional results.

Most of all, I want to thank my family who has been the greatest source of teaching of all. To my parents and grandparents, who somehow instilled this endless thirst to learn in my soul. While I talk about my likenesses and differences with them, I love them deeply and am blessed to have been born into their family. To Eileen, my awesome wife and life partner, who has taught me the magic of what happens when you lock the escape hatch.

Introduction

What is "Little Voice Mastery"?

"The path to success isn't as long as most people think."

—Blair Singer

Every day, we hear and read stories of people who have risen above the murkiness of mediocrity to enjoy fame and fortune. In the blink of an eye, they simply make the decision to "go for it" and achieve success in the face of overwhelming odds. How does that happen?

An elderly woman in one of my sales and leadership programs stood before a room of more than two hundred people, as she struggled with shyness and the speech impediment she had suffered from her entire life. Finally, she took a deep breath, stood up straight, and delivered a speech that brought the entire room to tears. Power radiated from her entire body! The breakthrough not only shocked the room, but amazed her as well. Her life changed forever. How did that happen?

Can change happen for you that quickly? Can it happen for your finances, for your health, for your relationships, and even for the rest of your life?

The answer is YES, if you can learn to control the little voice in your brain. You know the little voice that I'm talking about? It's the thing inside your head that just said, "What little voice? I don't have a little voice!" That's the one! We all have one. If you are like me, you probably have more than one! The real questions are, which one of those voices is the "real me" talking, and which one will give me the success that I want?

We were all meant to be great in some way—all of us, and that includes YOU. Acknowledging and managing the little voices that fill your head is the key to being amazingly successful in all areas of your life.

As an author, speaker, and business owner, I have watched thousands of good people parade through motivational seminars and programs. Many of them walk away momentarily inspired, but after the euphoria wears off, the "real world" seems to cave back in on them. They ultimately walk away from those motivational experiences inspired by the speaker's strength and ability to overcome adversity, but now with an assumption that they also have to somehow become "superhuman" in order to achieve success. Or they think they have to have lived through some horrible personal, financial, physical, or emotional adversity to be motivated enough to become successful.

Does that mean you have to screw up that big to win? Do you have to have had so much bad stuff hanging on you that the only way out is up? You hear story after story of great life-changing moments, and it's as if change for the better can only come from a mountain of misery or some cataclysmic decision. What if my story or your story isn't like that? What if we're just normal folks? Do I have to invent misery to succeed?

Or, on the flipside, perhaps you've watched someone who is incredibly smart or gifted—a great athlete or celebrated thinker. Maybe he or she even had some tough times, but had enough talent to lift himself or herself out of that adversity and into greatness. You may think you haven't had a great idea in your life and that since you can't hang on the rim, your talent quotient is too low. But I'm here to tell you that's simply not true.

The premise of this book is that the path to success isn't as long as you think. People are typically bad judges of distance. The distance to success is only the distance between your right ear and your left ear. It's not years, months, or decades down the road. The path is found in your own head right now, and navigating it is simply about knowing how to manage the little voice in your head.

The book is entitled *Little Voice Mastery,* but the process to get to mastery is really learning to manage that little voice. That is the process you will learn.

This book is designed to show you how to find that path and get on to your ultimate success. It will dust you off, stand you up, give you a hug or a kick, whichever is appropriate, and send you out there to realize your brilliance in a very physical and tangible way.

Most of all, this book is dedicated to the spirit in you that has been waiting for a very long time to fly.

Part 1

Revealing and Mastering Your Little Voice

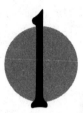

Gaining Control
of Your "Little Voice"

After more than twenty-five years of personal development teaching and train-ing, I have divided the world into two groups of people: the conscious and the unconscious. Those who are unconscious continue to plod along believing that the world is "doing it to them," that everything they see, hear, or read must either be true or a total conspiracy and that they are simply pawns in life. Conscious people, however, have the ability to step outside themselves and see themselves as instruments of *cause,* rather than simply at the *effect* of someone else's actions. The truth is, the minute you can step outside yourself and look at yourself objectively, that's when little voice mastery starts.

It's really about being able to step outside of your brain and look at the battle being fought there. It's about looking at it objectively and thinking, "That's inter-esting. Where did that thought, feeling, or impulse come from?" The minute you are able to separate yourself from your own psychoses (and believe me, we all have them!), then you're free. Most of the time, you're in too deep, too engulfed by them to see things clearly. You may actually believe that everything your little voice says is true. That it is all about your kids screaming, about money, about relationships, your health, your job, your boss. All that stuff. You are so "in it" that you are actually driven by it.

Yet the minute you say, "Hold it! That's my little voice talking, not necessarily the real me!" That's the minute you become conscious—that is when you are free. At that point, the real you has pulled away from your "own junk" and you are now looking at yourself from an objective view. That's very cool!

Now that's not to say you won't get sucked back into it again at some point. I don't think you are ever going to squash the little voice, fix all your neuroses, or become the epitome of enlightenment.

The minute you can step outside yourself and look at yourself objectively, is when little voice mastery starts.

So don't worry ... you don't have to become a saint to succeed. Also, success is not reserved for those who have overcome major trauma in their lives. Nor is it reserved for the gifted. (Although later I will show you that you *are* one of those gifted folks!)

I look at my own life. I don't come from any horrific background; it was pretty normal and drama-free. School was fine ... not great. I wasn't a straight-A student, but I did okay. I played sports. I was no star athlete, but I did all right. I was competitive at some things, and in some things I was a complete klutz. I don't come from a completely dysfunctional family. My parents have been married fifty years. That's pretty good. It's been stormy sometimes, but nothing unusual.

I have had a divorce, but so have 60 percent of Westerners. I've lost money and so has nearly everybody else. So what's the difference? I think the difference is that I'm willing to go up on stage and tell 15,000 people at a time that I know I've screwed up!

I'm willing to say to anybody that the only thing
that stands between me and what I want
is between my right ear and my left ear.

At some point, I realized that the money I had made and lost, the relationships that had worked and died, and all of the other success and nonsense that had happened in my life, all had one thing in common. You know what it was? Me! I know you're thinking, "No kidding, you idiot!" But at the time, when I came to that conclusion, it was a major revelation. I had known it intellectually, but until I truly got it physically and emotionally, I was not in control. Then I got it.

When I relate this to others, they think it's funny and they laugh, but in fact, most people know what I mean. They've been through similar revelations themselves. Even so, what stops them from succeeding is their own inability to step outside of a situation and see it objectively. They're both admiring and sympathetic to anyone else who can admit they've screwed up, yet they're scared to admit it openly about themselves. And by the way, when I say "screwed up," I mean it in the best way possible.

By admitting to your own shortcomings, you can recognize that we all have problems ... some uglier than others, but most of them pretty normal. The minute you can identify it and admit it, you are free to do or be what you want. At that point, you are now conscious—you are at cause, not at the effect. You are no longer victimized by your own brain.

Years ago, as a sales rep and later as a business owner, I became relentless about my attempts to clean up my head and sort out my issues. I figured that the more I focused on clearing up my own issues, the more money I would make and the more successful I would eventually become. And it worked! But, as you clean up smaller issues, you often uncover bigger ones. For example, when I started in sales, I couldn't make a cold call to save my life.

In the process of handling that issue, I realized that my real problem was my fear of looking stupid (sound familiar?), and that the only way to deal with it was to face it enough times until it was no big deal.

But as the groups of people got bigger, I realized that I had an even bigger fear of public humiliation and embarrassment! However, because I knew that big wins came from big groups, I forced myself to deal with that issue, too. Now I routinely speak in front of thousands of people.

But it doesn't end there. Sometimes the reward for solving a challenge is a bigger challenge! How big of a business could I build? How great of a family could I have? How difficult of an issue could I confront and master? How many millions of people could I touch? As I handle the fears and worries that come with each of those challenges, everything accelerates.

As you take on bigger tasks, you sometimes unlock bigger fears that show up in the form of your little voice. By stepping outside of yourself and handling those little voice issues, you are free to play a bigger game with more money, better relationships, and greater satisfaction.

R. Buckminster (Bucky) Fuller, the great author, philosopher, architect, and inventor once said that true leadership comes from "the willingness to be able to admit publicly to your mistakes." Being willing to say, "Yeah, I've screwed up and I'm the first to admit it," is a major step toward overcoming little voice interference, not to mention becoming a great role model for others.

The *"Little Voice" Mastery Systems CD—20 Ways to Reprogram Your Brain in 30 Seconds or Less*, I call my $500,000 CD, because that is easily what I've spent in the last twenty-seven years on personal development training, books, tapes, counseling, coaching, clearing, and processing for myself.

Good news: You don't have to spend all of that money or take nearly that long. We are going to get a giant chunk of it handled right here in this book, right now! If I have one gift, it is the ability to take what I have learned and create powerful, permanent shortcuts for others so that they can get what they want quickly.

Are you up for it? A great example of the power of "little voice" mastery is my friend Robert Kiyosaki. You would know him as the best-selling author of

Rich Dad Poor Dad. We have been friends for almost thirty years. One of the reasons we have remained friends for so long is because we are both relentless about dealing with that little voice in our own heads.

One of the reasons that his book *Rich Dad Poor Dad* has been so popular is because, while Robert talks about his Rich Dad and his Poor Dad, he's also talking about the rich little voice and the poor little voice, the winner and the loser inside each of us. The reason that book is so compelling and has sold so many copies is because it resonates with so many people. They can relate to the idea that inside everyone is a rich person and a poor person, a winner and a loser, a success and a failure.

The people who become the most successful are those who realize this internal battle is going on and do whatever it takes to win that battle.

The bottom line is that everyone can do this. Most importantly, YOU can do this! You can be successful. Cracking the nut of success means having the ability to say, "This is *my* little voice talking. This is *my* issue, *my* dilemma, *my* demon." To understand what is driving you—good, bad, or otherwise—to be able to recognize it when it pops up, take positive, corrective action, and apply the appropriate little voice mastery technique … that's what makes you successful.

People say that money, success, and relationships aren't necessarily what life is all about. And that may be true. But ironically, the quest for money, success, and relationships, and even health are what tend to flush up the little voices that block you.

That's why it is imperative that you score your progress in life not just by how you feel, but by what you physically create in the real world. It will measure your success in the battle of your brain and in your ability to serve yourself and others.

You are who you are, for better or worse. I believe that just about everyone is a good person—or at least we start out that way. Every child is born with a pure heart and a fresh spirit in the beginning. What happens after that is another issue.

All of your experiences make you into who you are today. So as you look into the mirror, what part of the reflection are you happy with and which part would you like to change?

- Are your finances the way you want them to be?
- Does your body look the way you want it to?
- Are your kids the kids you want them to be?
- Are you hanging out with the people you really want to?
- Is your job or career in the place you want it to be?
- Do you feel the way you want to every day?

When you look into your own eyes, what are they telling you? Take a look!

Cracking the nut of success means having the ability to say, "This is my little voice talking. This is my issue, my dilemma, my demon."

It may be a bit direct, but you have to start the conversation by telling the truth. You may be in better shape than you think.

In any case, the secret to regaining the power, strength, and brilliance that you want is simply by dealing with your issues and your stumbling blocks as you encounter them. As I have witnessed with thousands of people over the years, the solving of each issue results in bigger rewards. What if I told you that it would only take seconds, not a lifetime, to handle them?

Having the willingness to face yourself in the heat of the battle is the hardest thing of all. Sometimes you have to put yourself in "the heat" in order to get to the truth. In the books *The ABC's of Building a Business Team That Wins* and *Standing in the Heat*, we talk about the necessity of applying pressure to create extraordinary results. It's called perturbation.[1] The key word here is "perturb"!

---

[1] Perturbation is defined as "upsetting the status quo." When pressure is added to a system, it can transform into a more complex and stronger entity. Wood can become coal, which then can become diamond.

We don't typically like things that perturb us, and sometimes the biggest perturbation of all is admitting the truth to yourself, that sometimes you are an idiot. There are those who can do this easily and painlessly. There are others who are unwilling to humble themselves this way. But the biggest problem is those who feel they are always idiots and are therefore incapable of doing anything.

There's one thing that you must understand: it's not *you* who is an idiot. It's your little voice, which is convincing you that you are. I guarantee you that for every time you've felt like an idiot, there's also a time when you've felt like a legend in your own mind. The question becomes: which one is right, or what's the truth? Because your subconscious doesn't know the difference between fact and fiction!

If you were really an idiot, you would never have felt like a legend. You would never have had those awesome moments or those peak experiences in your life. You also would never have picked up this book! So we know that you're not REALLY an idiot. But there may be a little voice in your brain right now telling you that you are. The only sane way to operate, therefore, is to know that somewhere inside there is a wonderful, talented spirit that really can do great things.

I think that everyone is programmed to do something great. Not everyone follows through, and not everyone figures that out, but they could. Each time you mess up, you move another step closer to that inborn greatness. As Bucky Fuller said, "Mistakes are how human beings learn. You were given a right foot and a left foot ... not a right foot and a wrong foot. You correct to the right, then to the left and to the right again and ultimately move forward." It's not "messing up"; it's a "learning experience."

> *The challenge is to find out what you are supposed to do*
> *and get on with doing it ...*
> *but you will only find it through trial and error.*

In the process of that quest, each time you have a learning experience, all of your little voices are going to come up, particularly the ones that say, "You're not good enough," "You're not smart enough," or "You're not good-looking enough."

Or sometimes it's the little voice that questions you: "Am I making the right decision? Am I doing the right thing? Am I out of my mind? Why am I doing this?"

Introspection is something that all great leaders do—they are always questioning themselves. All successful persons I have ever talked to, at some level, thinks that they are a little crazy. (See? You're in good company.) They're always fighting that internal battle with their little voices. Eventually, one side or the other has to win. It's like in the movie *Boiler Room*, where Ben Affleck's character Jim Young says:

> *"There is no such thing as a 'no sale' call. A sale is made on*
> *every call you make. Either you sell the client some stock,*
> *or he sells you on a reason he can't. Either way, a sale is made.*
> *The only question is ... who's gonna close? You or him?"*

It's a powerful message because he is absolutely right. Especially if I say it this way: There is no such thing as a "no sale" call. A sale is made on every call you make. (Including the ones to yourself!) Either you sell yourself on the reason why you take action, or you sell yourself on a reason why you won't. Either way, a sale is made. The only question: which part of you will close—the winner or the loser?

So when do I let the loser win, and when do I let the winner win? Being able to win that battle is what it takes to be successful. I don't think superior talent, facing great adversity, or having a great stroke of genius is required.

The secret to success does not lie in being stoic, or having a "stiff upper lip," or any of that nonsense. There was a day and age when that may have been true, but I think our way of life is far too complicated for that now. The choices you have are much greater than they used to be. You have to move faster and be more nimble, more flexible, and more intuitive. There's no time to be stoic ... you've gotta change and move!

You are much more evolved than others who came before you. You came into this world with abilities and knowledge that your parents and grandparents didn't have. You're able to make certain assumptions that fifty years ago would have seemed outlandish. Humans are more intelligent and evolved now than ever before.

For example, when you talk about putting a person on the moon, it's a big deal to me. I remember the event! Then talk to my fifteen-year-old son, or a twenty-five-year-old about putting a person on the moon, and they'll say, "Yeah, so what?" They've moved on to higher levels of expectation.

Introspection is something that all great leaders do—they are always questioning themselves.

If there is a purpose in life for human beings, it is probably to be able to deal with more complex issues—not less complex ones—to solve problems. Have you ever noticed that once you solve a problem, your next problem is always bigger? And in business, the bigger the problem you solve, the more money you make when you solve it.

By the way, complexity is not the same as stress. Stress is an emotional response to the complexity if the wrong little voices take over or if you don't know how to manage them.

Why does that happen?

Somewhere along the way, we were taught to believe that you have to have all the answers to be smart or successful, and that the person who knows the most is smarter, better, and stronger. WRONG!!! That world doesn't exist. That's why you feel stress. Because you were programmed to believe that you have to be able to "figure it all out" and if you can't, you're stupid.

You know what intelligence *really* is? It's your ability to sense, intuit, and feel, to see patterns and develop relationships, connections, and associations to events, people, and circumstances. That's true intelligence. You didn't learn that in school because you already knew how to do it. Yet the little voice inside you still got programmed to look for the right answers, and when it can't always find them, it freaks out!

That gap between exercising true intelligence and the subconscious need to have the right answers is what creates the stress, and in stressful situations, that doubting little voice can get the upper hand.

Here's what I believe:

You are supposed to deal with greater complexity, not more stress.

Mastering little voice management reduces the stress, so that dealing with greater complexity is more fun and more lucrative. It's like playing a bigger game, with better players and more options. It's like getting better and better at the game and wanting to advance in it.

In that mode, you don't want to make the game simpler. You want it to be more challenging; otherwise, there's no reason to play. Think about any downloadable games in which the goal is always to get to higher and higher levels of complexity. Each level requires greater levels of mastery, and in turn, you develop more confidence. You don't want to go backward. You want to go forward. It's natural. You want to play the game faster, and you blaze through the simpler levels just so you can get to the good part. But somehow, in life, our acceleration toward increased complexity struggles. It's not about your brain capacity—it's your little voice!

Inside you, there's a champion and a loser. There's an angel and a devil. There's a hero and a villain. You have them all inside of you. The question is, which one is going to win today? Do you even *know* which one is controlling you right now?

Once you can identify them, you can then successfully manage them. No matter who you are, I suspect that you know there is an even bigger, better person inside you. That's true for me, too. But what stands in the way of that person fully emerging? How do you go from Point A, where you are now, to Point B, which is being the most powerful, passionate, wealthy, and healthy person you know? For me, what stands in my way is me! And I know it's the same for you. This book will give you the tools to get to Point B fast!

In the book *SalesDogs,* we said, "You don't have to be an attack dog to be successful." Everybody has a talent; everybody has a different way of being successful—as a poodle, a basset hound, or a retriever. It doesn't really matter which one of the other dogs you are. Everybody has something valuable to offer. So why don't we offer it? What's the resistance?

For example, your internal conversation may start like this: "Why don't you start your own business? You have always wanted to do it."

Then the resistance shows up like this nagging chatter of voices, saying things like: "Well, because you're not smart enough. You don't know how to set up a business. You'll starve to death if you try to do that. It's too risky."

Inside you, there's a champion and a loser. There's an angel and a devil. There's a hero and a villain. The question is, which one is going to win today?

So what causes this? Perhaps you have lost the ability to value yourself, your ideas, and your abilities because you have fallen into the trap of comparing yourself to others. With every success story that the media churns up, with every achievement you see "the other guy" get, you either become challenged or depressed.

And so, you don't start the program for kids that you constantly think about or write that book you've dreamed of writing, because you don't value what you have to offer. You think you aren't smart enough or that what you're offering won't be good enough. You say to yourself:

"I'm not successful enough myself."

"I'm not a good enough business person."

"I don't know how to write a book."

"I'm too old."

"I can't."

"I don't know how, and even worse, my information is not that good,
 not that new."

"It's not that different."

"I'm too tired."

"Who's going to read it?"

"I'm too young."

"Nobody's going to like it."

"Who wants to hear from me?"

You have the dream, but there seems to be resistance. That little voice starts
creating big old blocks to achieving your dreams. Stuff comes up, robbing you of
the time you would spend on your dream. Other things take greater priority. You
get tired. You procrastinate. Sound familiar?

It becomes more important to clean out your garage than to sit down and write
a book, because no one is going to read it anyway.

This book is about valuing yourself. It's about overcoming the little voice in
your brain that says you aren't up to the task at hand. You are going to learn how
to rehabilitate yourself and assess your value properly. Once you do, your value
will grow.

If you don't have people on your team, it's because you don't acknowledge and
value other people enough. If your health isn't good, it's because you don't value
yourself enough. If you don't have enough money in your life, it's because you have
lost your ability to determine value and you're being cheap someplace else in your
life. If you're going to be cheap on yourself, other people are going to be cheap

with you. You act as a magnet, attracting the same things to you that you're putting out there.

The reason many people never get to their dreams is because they are losing the ultimate "little voice battle" being waged in their brains. I'm talking about their assessment of themselves and who they are: their worthiness, their abilities, and whether they have anything to offer that anybody else would be interested in. Why would somebody want a cheap hamburger? Why would anyone pay more than fifty cents for a cup of coffee? See where I'm going with this? I could go on and on, but understand that it's all about your own perceived value.

Everybody has something to give, something to offer, even if it's already been offered before. *You* have a different way of looking at it. Your idea may appeal to millions of people you've never met before who think the way you think.

That's why it's important to get a handle on managing your "little voice"—so that ultimately, you can make your dream come true and put your idea out to the world for other people to appreciate and benefit from. Resistance is just "little voice" stuff standing in your way. Let's handle it, shall we?

What is the "Little Voice" and Whose is It Anyway?

This is a question I hear a lot. People ask, "What's this 'little voice'?"and I say, "It's that chatter that goes on in your brain."

Some say, "I don't have a little voice." Well, you do; we all do. Mine happens to sound like my mother. I don't know what yours sounds like. Sometimes it can be very high-pitched, sometimes whiney, and sometimes scoldy!

Whatever your little voice says usually sounds logical and reasonable. That's the problem. Because it sounds so logical, you have a tendency to listen to it too much, and sometimes you end up believing it. Your little voice is really the sum of all the experiences and advice you have had in your life that you don't spend much time actively thinking about. *+ evolutionary Solving problem brain need -*

You see, you have both a conscious mind and a subconscious mind. I call it sub-conscious because although we have thousands of memories in our brains, we

17

don't necessarily think about them all the time. But those memories rise to the surface the second the right "trigger" arrives. For example, have you ever been heartbroken? Have you ever lost money? Have you ever loaned money to somebody, and they didn't pay you back? If you didn't say "yes" to at least one of those three questions, you're probably lying. The good thing is that we don't think about those experiences every day.

The way the little voice works in your everyday life is a bit like this: Let's say that you and I have been working together for a couple of months. Everything is really great and we have a good relationship. One day, I come up to you and say that I am a little short on cash. If you could loan me some money, I'll pay you back.

Now, if you have been burned before, immediately a little voice in your head screams, "Oh yeah! Last time that happened, I got stung! You can't trust people. No way!"

That response surfaced out of the subconscious. Something in the real world today, like my request for the money, shook it loose. My innocent request triggered a prior experience or set of experiences that had some volatile emotions attached to it. At that point, the little voice gave you a warning message.

And here is the tragic part of this scenario. Even though we may have had a great relationship, maybe for months or even years, it can be destroyed in an instant. Suddenly, you don't trust me as much. You feel a need to create more distance between us. You don't see me the same way. The relationship is all of a sudden deteriorating, and yet it has nothing to do with me!

It has to do with an old memory of yours and the negative emotions that are attached to that memory. You end up projecting those negative feelings onto me, and our relationship may never be the same because your little voice jumped in and changed things. That is, unless you deal with it.

This is one of the dangers of listening to your little voice indiscriminately—your tendency to believe that everything it says is true. Your little voice is only some leftover, unresolved issue or series of issues from your past. But because of it, you could be missing out on a great personal relationship, or a genuinely lucrative business opportunity. Something similar could happen in relation to your health or myriad other things. But the fact remains, many potentially great opportunities can be marred or negated completely by that little voice if it's left unchecked.

> *Your "little voice" is simply the subconscious* ~~Dreams Cycles~~
> *part of your brain that talks to you.* ~~Trances~~ !

When I was a kid I'd watch Mickey Mouse cartoons, and there were always two characters who would each sit on one of Mickey's shoulders. One was the little red devil, and the other was the pure white angel. The devil would say, "Yeah! Go ahead and break the rules. Go for it. It's okay to do it!"

Meanwhile, the angel would say, "No! Keep away. Be good. Don't cause trouble. Do the right thing." It was a constant battle between them, an angel and a devil fighting each other. Disney gave us a great way to visualize what the battle is like between the little voices in our head.

The little voices are not necessarily good, and they are not necessarily bad. It's just that they lie dormant until they get triggered.

Also, there's a difference between the little voice that robs you of success and the voice that tells you not to make irrational decisions without due diligence.

Years ago, while I was living in Hawaii, I came across an opportunity to invest in some land overlooking Kealakekua Bay, on the Big Island. It was around $10,000 for about five acres of land with a commanding view of the coast. Ten thousand dollars, in those days, was not a huge amount of money, but it was substantial for me at the time. The fact of the matter was that six months earlier, I had been burned on a similar deal in Colorado. I had lost all the money I'd invested in that property, and when this opportunity in Hawaii came along, I was still a bit raw from that experience. Because of my prior experience, I looked at that Hawaii property and that little voice inside my head said, "No! You're going to get burned again. It's too risky. You know what's going to happen, blah, blah, blah," and I let it go.

That piece of property today has been subdivided. Those one-acre lots have each been developed, have sold several times, and are worth millions.

That was a long time ago, and a lot has transpired since then. But that is what the little voice can do to you—it can cause you to miss out on something really great. If I had only realized that I was the problem, and not the property, I may have made a different decision. Sure, I need to be more diligent. Yes, I need to ask more questions and do more research. But I shouldn't take myself out of the game entirely! Before making a decision, I need to understand whether my fear is based on issues from the past or just simple common sense.

I can give you countless similar situations, and as you read this, I'm sure you can come up with your own. I've seen it happen in relationships and in business dealings, where one little voice was battling with the other. One said "Do it," and the other said, "Don't do it." Typically, the little voice that holds you back from success is the one telling you not to do something: Don't make an investment. Don't take a chance. Don't step out of your comfort zone. Don't set yourself up for embarrassment or loss.

In my experience, whenever that voice is telling me *not* to seize an opportunity, that's when I have to take a look and say, "Where is that little voice coming from? Is it coming from an emotion? Where did that emotion come from? Where have I experienced that before? What is the *real* issue?"

If I can go back to whatever created the emotion or fear to begin with, it no longer controls me. I can make a conscious decision based upon the reality of the moment, rather than an unconscious one based upon fear of repeating the past. If I can do that, the little voice I can then hear is the *real* me. It's really that simple.

This is what I work on when I go to my own personal development training and coaching mentors—Jayne Johnson, Kim White, Mack Newton, and Alan Walter's team. These are people I go to when I seem to be encountering the same "little voice" problem over and over again. At those times, something is going on between my right and left ears, preventing me from going to the next level. These people know how to ask the right questions, to lead me back to where that little voice first started its ranting, so I can control it.

So, whose little voice is it? It's mine. It's yours. But it can be a lot of other people's voices, too—your parents, your teachers, your friends, your spouse, family members—people with good intentions, trying, in many cases, to protect you by telling you what to do. They say things like, "Money doesn't grow on trees," or, "If you can't afford it, don't buy it," or perhaps you were fortunate to be taught to ask yourself, "How *can* you afford it?"

Your little voices will then ask similar questions, too. If you come from a family of employees, of self-employed people, people who were cautious, or people who never made investments, then your little voice will be an amalgam of all the advice those people have ever given you.

As for me, I love my extended family. But in the time I spend with them, I don't talk much about investments, business, or even politics because my views are very different from theirs. I find that those conversations trigger emotions inside of me and in them. It's not because of them. It's because of the little voice conditioning that I had while being in their presence growing up and my decision since then to create a different life for myself.

One of the things I'm glad I did early on in my life was going away to college after I graduated from high school. My college was over three hours away from home, so I lived on campus. Then, when I graduated from college, I moved to Hawaii. In my mind, it was as far away from Ohio, where I grew up, as I could possibly get. My parents were very upset by my decision to go so far away, and they repeatedly tried to convince me to move back, but I didn't.

I stayed in Hawaii for eight years. Then I went to California, then Arizona, Lake Tahoe, and then Arizona again. I always kept plenty of distance between who I was in the past and where I am today. Why? Is it because I don't love my family? Absolutely not. I love my family dearly. But the environment in which I grew up and the conditioning I received were preparing me to be someone's employee, or someone who was self-employed and worked alone. And that's not who I am, or who I ever wanted to be.

Growing up, my little voice told me that I needed to go out and get a safe, secure job, or to become a self-employed professional and earn lots of money for myself. But deep in my heart of hearts, I always wanted to build a business.

In the beginning, I had tremendous trouble achieving my goals because my little voices were freaked out by uncertainty. I had to learn to face risk, deal with the fears, get my head around complexity, and put all the right elements together to make things work. The business deals and investments were never the hard thing. The real battle was the one in my brain. I found that the more distance I could get from my past conditioning, the easier everything became.

Your "little voices" are really the sum of all the experiences and advice you have had in your life.

Don't get me wrong. I see my family a lot, and we are very close. They are all great people, but we live in different worlds. Our missions and goals are different—not right or wrong, simply different.

I've heard people say that you are a reflection of the six people you spend the most time with. If that's true, and you look at that over the period of a lifetime, you will find that many of your thoughts are reflections of theirs, particularly if you have spent a lot of time with them and you respect them. You cannot help but be affected by them.

So, whose little voice is it? Part of it is yours. Parts belong to your mom, your dad, your teachers ... you name it. But ultimately, it's yours and how you've been affected by other people.

That's not always a bad thing. I had great coaches growing up that taught me endurance, leadership, and tenacity. My father taught me integrity and values. My mom taught me love. My grandfather taught me negotiations and entrepreneur-ship. But in order to fully reach my potential, I needed to embrace only those thoughts that would empower me, and leave behind those thoughts that held me back.

We are influenced by others and by life's experiences. And it's completely up to you to respond to those experiences. For example, if you're thinking about making an investment and everybody tells you it's a great deal, everyone's doing it, go for it,—you might do it. And say you end up losing a ton of money. Your little voice might caution you against similar investments in the future. But it's about how you respond to that voice that will determine your future. You might say, "I'll never do that again." Or you might, depending on your influences, say, "Based on what I've learned, I'm going to dig deeper into this so that I know what I am doing next time. I can't wait for the next opportunity so I can redeem myself!!!" Again, it's up to you to determine which little voices win.

How you respond to any given incident has a lot to do with your own mental conditioning and emotional strength. If you are strong emotionally, you'll take a more aggressive approach. You are willing to handle a little more risk. You'll be willing to try again. You'll be willing to bounce back with new energy. If you are emotionally beaten up, the negative little voice is likely going to win. It will say things like, "Back off. I told you not to do that type of thing."

As for whose little voice it is, I wish I could say it's just yours, but it's not. It belongs to everybody in your life that has had an influence on you, people whom you revere, and maybe some you don't. Ultimately, however, the goal is for you to not only understand whose little voice it is, but to be able to clearly hear the little voice that is the real you—the passionate, optimistic, talented, and unaffected you!

There's a little voice inside of you that REALLY knows what to do. It's the one that knows what's best for you and can help you to grow.

Most living things want to grow. As a matter of fact, I think the passion to grow is at least as great as the desire to protect. There is an appropriate time for each.

There is a part of you, your spirit, that is the ultimate little voice, the one that is truly you. It's the little voice that says things like, "This is your gift. This is what you are supposed to be doing. No matter what, don't let anybody take this away from you. You know you can do this. Keep going. You're good. You're honest. You're brilliant. This is you. Keep going." I think everybody hears that little voice once in a while. Deep down, that's really who you are!

You have the ability and the insight to recognize that little voice, your true spirit or essence, if you want to call it that—the part of you that was meant to be a brilliant, wealthy master of some gigantic game, someone able to accomplish great things.

There are moments in everyone's life, (for some it happens every day!) when you feel like you could play, and win, one of those gigantic games. You feel like a legend in your own mind and your little voice is saying, "That's how you make a sales call!" or "Yeah, let's do this deal." It may only be a $1,000 deal, but you walk out of there thinking, "This is awesome!!! See ... I told you that you were going to be rich!!!" Your little voice goes crazy, it's so excited. My experience is that that is your true little voice. That is the little voice that is you—your spirit. Because you *can* play that big.

Every one of us has the capability of playing and winning a big game. Not everyone will. Little voices will determine the outcome. Other people's advice, worries, jealousy, resentment, and even their neuroses will stand in your way if you let them.

I don't think I've ever met anyone who didn't truly believe, at some point, that they could play a bigger game, close a bigger deal, have a greater influence, be a better parent, have better health, make more money, or have a greater impact at some point in their life. I know in the programs I conduct, whether it's sales training, team training, or personal development training, the objective is always to get people to feel good about who they are. And generally, when people feel their most confident and optimistic, they're listening to that genuine voice, the one they were born with that constantly pushes them to succeed.

Bucky Fuller says all people were born geniuses, and I believe that. As you grow, however, you start listening to your relatives, your peers, people who claim to be experts, and the blizzard of advice that the media throws at you. And as you listen, you start to absorb and echo their thoughts. Their voices may be trying to protect you, but the point is that their voices don't belong to you.

Bucky Fuller told the story of how his life had taken several bad turns: The death of his youngest daughter, the failure of his business and the public scorn that came with it. It got so bad that ultimately his little voice drove him to the shores of Lake Michigan, where he had decided to swim out and let those churning waters take his life. But all of a sudden, another little voice in his head started speaking, and here is what it said:

"You don't have the right to eliminate yourself.
You don't belong to you. You belong to the universe.

Your (true) significance may remain forever obscure (a mystery)
to you, but rest assured that you are fulfilling your purpose
if you commit yourself to the highest advantage of others."

He realized that he had been put here for some greater task. A task to serve others. He went on to create inventions, architecture, and a methodology of thinking that served all of humanity. Time magazine called him the "gentle genius" of our times. Those words from his little voice, his own little voice, not only inspired him, but they have inspired thousands of others since that fateful day on the shores of Lake Michigan. The real little voice won!!

Bucky's story and message has resonated with me for years. I believe that deep down inside most of us is the knowledge and understanding that we have greatness. You do have something to give. You do belong to the universe, and you were put here for a reason. And that reason may not be clear to you now, but if you pay attention, you will get clearer.

This doesn't mean you have to change the planet or the course of history. But maybe you'll invent something. Maybe you'll raise great kids that turn into great leaders. Maybe you'll touch people in a way that changes their lives. Maybe you'll show others how to be financially free, emotionally nourished, or physically vibrant. The point is, we owe it to ourselves, and in fact to the world, to sort out our true voice from the 2,500 other voices that may be rattling around inside our brain, so that we can do what we're ultimately meant to do.

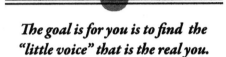

The goal is for you is to find the "little voice" that is the real you.

In Bucky's case, he realized that all those negative thoughts in his head were not really his own. In fact, they belonged to his grandparents and his uncles, who had been trying for so long to tell him what to do and how to conduct his life. And while they meant well, those voices only got him in trouble, because their advice didn't fit with his life. Sound familiar?

As he stood there at the water's edge, he said to himself, "I had better start thinking for myself." And do you know what he did? He took a two-year vow of silence! That's right. For two years he wouldn't talk to anybody, and he didn't allow anyone to talk to him. He did this in order to clear his mind and think what he wanted to think.

For me, this was an incredibly powerful message, one that forced me to ask myself, "Whose little voice is this, anyway? Which one is mine, and what are my thoughts?"

Right now, as you read this book, what thoughts are you having? Ask yourself whether those thoughts are really yours. If they're not, whose are they? You may not be able to answer that question right now, but the power comes in the asking. If you ask, you begin to take control of your own spirit once again. *You have to ask.* Every day, we are bombarded by so many messages, so much advice from so many people. We're assaulted by images of people, places, and things, politicians and sales pitches. It all makes thinking for yourself a difficult task.

Don't get me wrong. I'm not saying that you shouldn't turn to others for advice. But remember to hang on to the advice that truly supports who you are and what you really believe, the advice that encourages you to be who you're meant to be. Take the advice of those who are pushing you to succeed—to play a bigger game and to take on greater challenges. Take the advice of those who push you further on the path toward becoming whoever it is you're supposed to be. Only then will you begin to hear the real voice inside your head.

Periodically, I have to take a good look at my life and clear my head. That's why I constantly focus on personal development. If I get stuck on something and feel unable to take action, it's possible that there are thoughts in my head that aren't really mine. Or perhaps those thoughts are based on some past emotional experience that really isn't relevant today.

Many years ago, I went through a very painful, heartbreaking divorce. Later, I met someone else and got engaged, and again I got my heart broken. My relationships had come to resemble a bad soap opera. And so, logically, my little voice came to the conclusion that, "You just can't trust women!!!" (There's a brilliant thought!) Luckily I had great friends and mentors at the time who kept me focused and working on the real issues.

In fact, when I began to look at my history of heartache, I realized that it all began when I was jilted at the age of seventeen. The thought of "no trust" was not a new one. It was an old one and I had been operating every subsequent relationship based upon that little voice thought!

So when the next relationship came along, of course I experienced that same fear and lack of trust. And of course, it became a self-fulfilling prophecy. The relationship ended, as did the relationship after that. And every time it happened, that little voice got stronger and stronger, because there seemed to be overwhelming evidence for it. The problem was I was attracting it by believing that the voice in my head was *always true!!!*

That little voice was indeed mine, based upon my own experiences. But unfortunately, it was also based on one stupid moment in a very emotionally wrought time in my life. Heightened emotions yield low intelligence. How are you going to have any kind of relationship if you don't trust people? The idea that you can't trust an entire sex is, let's face it, ridiculous. But that's what happens when you operate under the naïve assumptions of a seventeen-year-old.

How many times have similar voices spoken to you, affecting your relationships, your money, or your life? Just remember to ask yourself where those voices originated. Once you do that, that little voice *will* eventually go away. And on those rare occasions when it rears its ugly head, you can simply say to it, "Thanks for sharing!" and move on without further distractions.

You don't have to listen to any of them. You don't have to think thoughts that you don't want. You don't have to eat anything that you don't want to eat. You don't have to spend time with anyone you don't want to spend time with. So when you hear voices you don't want to hear, say "Stop!" Tell your brain you don't want to hear them. If you do that often enough, those voices will disappear.

Trust me, there are days when I actually walk around saying, "STOP! STOP! STOP!" out loud. Anyone observing may think I'm crazy, but that's okay. It's more important that I stop and redirect my thinking. If I'm diligent enough about doing this, those negative thoughts won't rule me anymore.

> **You have been conditioned to be what you are. That means that you can also condition yourself to be who you want to be.**

The good news is that you will learn how to do this in seconds before we are all done! It's that easy!

At a recent presentations workshop, we ran drills in which everyone had to acknowledge the rest of the group of more than 300 people by saying something like this: "Thank you for coming today and spending your time with me. You have my commitment that I'll do everything in my power to make sure that it will be well worth your time and your effort."

One woman in the group, for some reason, couldn't seem to get through the statement, "You have my commitment." Every time she came to the word "commitment," her brain went blank. She would stutter or forget the words. Something about that word created a mental block for her. So instead of getting into some sort of emotional cross-examination, I simply had her repeat it over and over again, but each time, she became stuck. Finally, after about two minutes of this, she became disgusted with herself. You could see it on her face. Inside her head, her own little voice was saying, "Come on, this is ridiculous. Let's get on with it. We don't need to do this."

Finally, she took a deep breath, took two steps forward, and said, "You have my commitment that I'll do everything in my power to make sure that it will be worth your time and effort. Thank you for being here."

All 300 people stood up and gave her a standing ovation. Not only had she said it, but she had said it with such power and force that they were moved by it. So was she. With tears streaming down her cheeks, she realized that her fear of commitment and being in front of people had forced her to take a back seat to all the things she had REALLY wanted to say in the past .... all the great ideas that she WANTED to put on the table but had been afraid to present. In only a couple of minutes, she had overridden the little voice that had held her back. This is the power of the little voice. But with some coaching and proper repetition, that little voice can be reprogrammed in a matter of minutes.

You created the little voice, and *you* have the ability to change it.

You DO need advice about some things. And you do need good mentors. After all, you'd never jump out of an airplane without a parachute. Operating without advice or guidance won't help you to get any closer to your goals, and it may, in fact, hurt more than it helps. But the key is in separating the good advice and the good mentors from the bad. Are they pushing you toward your goals, or away? Are they pumping you up, or holding you back? You'll need to do some research to be sure the advice you receive is good.

You know one of the greatest things about getting older? As any older person will tell you, you start to care a heck of a lot less what people think of you. And that's a good thing, because one of the most powerful little voices in your brain is the one that worries about what other people think. I would even argue that in both your business and your personal life, this is the single most powerful, most debilitating little voice you have.

Years ago, I read a study that said the fear of public humiliation was greater than the fear of death. Death was number three on the list. Rejection by your peers was number two. Think about that. The two greatest fears are centered around what others may or may not think about you. Where does that come from?

Maybe it came from school, when you would raise your hand and give the wrong answer, and everyone would laugh at you. Or maybe it came from the first time you mustered up enough courage to approach that first "love-of-your-life" and they brushed you off while your "friends" chuckled. Wherever it came from, that little voice is keeping you from being the person you're supposed to be. When you're too concerned about what other people think, you make decisions based not on what's right for you, but on what's right for other people.

In Martin Luther King's final speech, which he made the day before he died, he said:

"I'm happy tonight. I'm not worried about any thing. I'm not fearing any man! Mine eyes have seen the glory of the coming of the Lord."

At that point in his life, he didn't care about what others thought. He was no longer afraid of what others might say or do to him. His "dream" or mission far outweighed the considerations that would slow him down, distract him, or discourage him. As a leader, he operated from a sense of mission first and self-interest last. That needs to be true for you, too, if you hope to accomplish the things you set out to do; your focus can't be on whether you look good or not, or whether or not everyone likes you.

If you take only one thing away from this book, if you tackle only one thing, let it be to manage or override the fear of what others may, or may not, think about you. Think about all the times in your life that you've held back, stopped your progress, or taken a back seat just because you were afraid of what others would think. Make a decision right now that you won't let that happen again.

You see, like most of us, you've been conditioned by some past, emotionally difficult experience, or by some bad advice. The best way to reprogram or manage it is to confront it head-on. Continue to put yourself in the line of fire, in front of people, over and over again until you become

> *Every one of us has the capability of playing and winning a big game. Not everyone will. Little voices will determine that outcome.*

comfortable. It may take time, but the more you expose yourself, the easier it becomes. The fear of what others think will become less and less controlling. Time does heal, but only if you practice.

So many people have ideas and dreams that don't come true because they're afraid to talk to people, afraid to put themselves out there and be bold and direct, afraid they're going to look like idiots. They believe too much is at stake in damaging their image. That fear of what others think, of embarrassment and rejection by your peers, could be the most critical issue in your life to handle. Remember this:

> **You should care about other people,
> but not about what they think about you.**

I urge you to do the following:

1. Watch or read Dr. King's final speech, and model it yourself. In other words, say it with the same facial expressions, body language, volume, accent, and energy as he did. Model him perfectly. Repeat it again and again, with the same passion as he had. Do it daily. You will find that you become bolder and stronger.

2. Practice handling objections by yourself, with a friend, or with a group of others who similarly want to learn how to be great communicators and negotiators. Your fear will subside.

3. Identify which little voices belong to you, and which debilitating one belong to other people. Make a list of where they each came from and what the experience was that created them. You will find it very freeing.

4. Ask yourself this question: If you had unlimited money and time, what would you do (after the vacations and partying) that would bring joy to your life, give you a sense of purpose, and would be advantageous to others? Perhaps that's what you should be doing now!

Managing Your
Little Voice Successfully

In the last chapter, we talked about whose little voices you are hearing in your head, which ones are yours and where they all came from. And most importantly, we talked about how understanding the source of each voice is one of the most liberating things you can do for yourself—because once you understand it, you can *manage* it.

I want to be really clear about this, because a lot of people ask me, "Can you really eliminate the little voice?" I don't think you ever *eliminate* it. And I wouldn't want to. There are times when those little voices are very important. They keep you from doing stupid, dangerous things, like jumping out of airplanes without parachutes. They kept you, as a little five-year-old, from crossing the street in front of an oncoming car. They push you to do adequate research before investing your time, money, or energy in a project.

So it's there for a reason. And most of those little bits of advice that you give yourself are good. The problem is that some of the advice you're used to hearing in your head is just habit. It's automatic now, and although it may have served you well in the seconds before crossing the street when you were five, that same advice may now be stopping you from getting on with other parts of your life.

You've listened to it for so long that you automatically let it seep into too many other parts of your life—situations that are unrelated to the simple situation of crossing a road. So you end up messing up a relationship, passing on a business deal, or avoiding risks that might be good for you. That's why you don't want to *eliminate* the little voice. The goal is to manage it.

Wouldn't it be great if you could just get all the negative chatter to just buzz off and stay in the background, while your positive thoughts push you ahead? We'd all be in much better shape. So, the first part of managing the little voice is to understand that you've got one. If you can step outside of yourself, acknowledge that conversation in your head, and ask yourself, "Where did that come from?" you are well on your way to managing it.

Most people are so used to listening to the racket of their little voice as part of their consciousness, they don't even realize the part that their little voice is playing in their lives, and therefore they can't step back and look at it objectively.

In high school, I used to run competitively. Some of my best races were when I was able to step outside of myself and actually watch myself run. Even when I was pushing so hard that I was in pain, I was able to somehow, in a sort of surreal way, step outside my body, or at least imagine doing so, and ask myself, "What's your form like, Blair? What's that other guy thinking? Lengthen your stride, loosen your upper body." This enabled me to perform better and, somehow, I was even able to gain a strange but powerful respect for myself. Even today, those moments give me renewed strength and energy.

Have you ever been walking down the street or driving in your car, and suddenly somebody in another car yells something offensive at you? Your little voice immediately reacts and starts yelling, "That stupid !@#$%!" or "Man, if I had the chance, I would really #$%&@# that guy!" You get so caught up in the heat of the moment, you don't have time to step back and detach yourself from that automatic response. It's almost like the "play button" in your brain got pushed, and the CD that's been sitting in there starts running automatically.

Certain stimuli will always create certain responses. For example, imagine that it's dinner time. The phone rings, and your caller ID shows you a number you don't recognize. You know it's some telemarketing company. Straight away, your brain reacts with, "Another pest! Someone trying to sell me something! I hate these people." And so you pick up the phone and you say, "I don't have time for this. We're eating dinner right now. Don't bother me again!" and you hang up the phone.

Now, that's an automatic response, based upon past experience. There's nothing wrong with that. The problem is that it's an automatic response. For all you know, it could be somebody calling on behalf of your sister or brother-in-law, using another phone for some reason, who needs to speak with you urgently. Now, I admit, the chances of that being the case are slim, but your brain's automatic response moved you right past a potential decision point, so you really had no choice but to react automatically. And unless you're able to step outside of yourself to manage the little voice, and say, "Wait a minute. What am I thinking right now? Why did I say that? Why am I doing this? Is this really the decision I want to make?" your response is already *pre-programmed!*

And that's good, in some cases. It'll keep you out of a bad business deal. It'll keep you from throwing away your money or causing bodily harm to yourself. But by the same token, if it's all *automatic, if you've already pre-wired it,* you're going to miss a lot of opportunities.

Experiences in the present can cause you to re-live negative feelings from the past, for example, where trust was betrayed, or money was lost, or feelings were hurt. In a way, your brain is like a computer. It's been trained to respond to certain triggers, and it uses shortcuts. All it may take is hearing someone say those two fatal words, "Trust me," and that big red "Danger" sign immediately goes up. You think, "Sure ... I've heard that one before." If it looks like a duck and sounds like a duck, it must be a duck, right? Well, this looks and sounds like another potential betrayal, and your pre-programmed response to that is, "No way! I'm not touching that with a ten-foot pole." You immediately take steps to get out of that situation any way you can. That betrayal CD has been pulled out of the response library and starts playing in your brain, and immediately you go on auto-response.

Remember my example at the beginning of the book: Someone whom you've had a great three-month relationship with asks you to loan him or her money? You hear "loan me money," the CD immediately gets pulled out of the drawer and put into the player, and that little voice automatically starts running. And without little voice management, that one comment can change a relationship forever.

I've seen work teams in which suddenly, out of nowhere, a comment, joke, question, or request changes everything. After three months, six months, or even a year of working together in a great relationship, someone's CD starts running automatically, and a whole series of responses based upon memories or past experiences begins to dictate the present and the future. The problem is that those responses were forged in the past, and may be inappropriate now. That's a case of no little voice management. That's operating on autopilot.

It can even be worse. In one of our programs, there was a very talented, middle-aged man who seemed to have a history of frustration at work. In spite of his talents, every time he approached his boss, he became timid and shy. This seemed to happen at every one of his jobs. While I found him to be engaging, creative, and energetic, when the subject of his boss came up, his shoulders would slump, his voice would drop, and his energy evaporated. Even though we were only discussing his situation, he was already on autopilot.

So in a role-playing situation, I pretended to be his boss, and I told him to ask me for a raise. He had a very tough time with it. For every objection I gave, he would shut down. Finally, I asked him how he felt. He said, "I feel intimidated." So I said, "Good! Now we're getting somewhere." At least he was able to observe himself.

I asked him when he had felt like that before. He said that it happened every time his boss came into the room. So I asked if he'd ever felt like this before his current boss came into the picture. To that he responded, "Yeah! My last boss, too!" So I asked when it had happened before any of that. He paused and cast his eyes downward. Suddenly his face became flushed. His eyes welled up with tears. He looked at me not through the eyes of a middle-aged man, but through the eyes of an intimidated eight-year-old boy. He said, "When my dad would scold me about my schoolwork." It was a huge moment for him.

His little voice was still running the same CD that got put into the library and started playing at age eight, when his old man ridiculed him at home. His boss was not his dad, and neither was I, but the little voice reacted to it in the same way nonetheless.

After this man experienced his "A-ha!" moment, I asked him if he could let go of that old response and start to see me not as his dad, but as who I was at that moment. A smile spread across his face, and through his tears he chuckled and said, "Yeah, I can give it a shot."

So we role-played it once again, and needless to say, his energy was over the top. His shoulders straightened, his face glowed. With confidence, he addressed each of my objections about giving him a raise. As the role-play continued, he created a simple plan to generate additional income for his company, the willingness to be 100 percent responsible for the plan, and the request to be compensated for some small percentage of the plan's profitability. It was brilliant.

I am sure that he had thought this through a hundred times, but the difference now was that he said it like a business owner, not like an employee, and certainly not like an intimidated one. When he had finished, everyone in the room cheered for him. In that moment, his success outside of the workshop was guaranteed. He told me later that not only did he get the raise, but he also finally realized that none of his bosses were the problem. The real problem had been the little voice that for so many years had been stuck on autopilot in his head. The moral of the story is that your life can change in a matter of minutes, once you gain control in the battle for your brain.

Has your emotion ever run high? I am sure it has. And you know that when you have emotion running high, your intelligence tends to run low. You say things that you don't really mean and sometimes even regret later. Ever happen? In those moments, when you finally catch yourself goofing up, have you ever smacked yourself in the head and wished you hadn't stuck your foot in your mouth? If you have ... you are practicing little voice mastery.

Not that I recommend smacking yourself in the head or saying stupid things. But the ability to say, "Stop! Whoa! Wait a minute! What did I say? I didn't mean to say that."—that's managing your little voice.

A lot of things in life trigger automatic and sometimes emotional responses. Let's say my wife and I are having a discussion about something, maybe the kids or our finances. Let's also say that I've had a bad day and I'm tired. And it also just so happens that in this conversation, my wife gives me a "look." (You know, "THE LOOK"!) My little voice interprets it as a challenge to my intelligence. (This never happens, right?) Obviously, I'm sensitive to that.

This turns out to be one of my "hot buttons," and left unmanaged, my CDs start jumping off the rack and playing at full volume. The next thing you know, I'm upset, I start making judgments, I get defensive, the discussion either deteriorates or ends all together. That's autopilot.

Instead of stopping for just a second and asking myself, "Why on earth am I getting so upset right now? This is ridiculous! It's just a facial expression!" I go straight into automatic response and either get angry or withdrawn. If I could just step outside of that situation for a moment, long enough to start asking myself some very basic questions, then I can begin to manage the little voice and keep from being taken out of the moment.

Later, we'll talk about actual physical, mental, and emotional techniques that you can use, so that when you realize that one of your "CDs" is starting to play, you'll know exactly what to say to yourself not only to stop it from automatically playing, but to redirect your thoughts in a positive direction, one that's more appropriately suited to the moment.

For myself, I know that my sensitivity to "the look" came from "the look" that I would get from my parents when they were disgusted with me for whatever reason. Once I could understand that, I could say, "Oh, that's a CD that's been running for a long time," and let it go.

You don't want to eliminate the little voice ... the goal is to manage it.

Remember that the minute you're able to step outside and look at your little voices objectively, those experiences from the past begin to lose their hold on you. And each time you recognize that same voice, you gain even more control over your reactions.

Here's the great news!! Where you are today is a result of years of programming.

But it only takes a very short time to de- or re- program yourself. It begins with self-awareness and objectively seeing yourself from the outside. Of course it's best to be able to do this in the heat of the moment, at the moment of reaction, but that's not always possible. (At least for me!) But even if you can do it ten minutes after a situation passes, that's still great. The next time it may only take five minutes, then maybe one minute, then thirty seconds, until you are back in control.

I'll give you another personal example. Recently I concluded a two-day program, after which several participants came up to me to pay me a compliment. In my head, the dialogue between these participants and my little voice went something like this:

Participant 1: "You know, I really appreciate the way you always do your best to build people up. I noticed you had people confront their issues. But you were gentle and it was very powerful."

My little voice: "Wow, that's awfully nice, but I don't know if I deserve all that credit."

Participant 2: "It was hugely confrontational for all of us, but every single person came out of it with a huge win, and no one ever felt demeaned in the process."

My little voice: "Okay, that's enough. I'm feeling uncomfortable with this."

Participant 3, 4, and 5: "It was great!" "Best program I've ever been to!"

"You changed my life!" "I want you to mentor me."

My little voice: "This is weird, and I want out of here."

Me (aloud to the group and to an assistant nearby): "That's great ... Hey, Kimberly, can I see you for a minute?"

In retrospect, however, I have to wonder, why did I have such a hard time taking a compliment? Why does it embarrass me so much? What CD does *my* head keep playing?

First of all, why do I even want to handle this situation in my brain? I can think of two reasons. First, have you ever met someone who could not handle success? They have this knack for always snatching defeat right from the jaws of victory. They simply cannot take a win. Self-deprecation may seem noble and a sign of humility, but an uncontrolled habit of that reduces confidence, creates anxiety, and creates doubt in moments you need the most energy and strength.

In some ways, there is a part of me that has been a bit like that. Can you relate? Much better to be able, when someone pays a compliment, to just say, "Thank you. Thank you very much. I appreciate that," and just enjoy feeling good about it, celebrate the win and build on it.

The second reason for managing this particular little voice is that it allows me to stay engaged and present with whoever is paying me the compliment, without blowing them off and making them feel that I don't acknowledge or appreciate them or their gratitude.

Right now, you might think I'm a nutcase, with all these little voice conversations going on inside my head. And okay, maybe I am. But if you're reading this book right now, I'm pretty sure you have them, too. Remember that the first step to an extraordinary life is to be honest about you to yourself.

So really, if at any point—no matter if it's a year later—you're able to look back at yourself and say, "Wow! What was I thinking?" you will have accomplished little voice management. Once you have regained control of your own mind, you're able to simply choose a new direction and move on.

The most important parts of little voice management are:

A. Being able to recognize that there's a little voice (or several!) in there

B. Being able to recognize that you must step outside and look at the voice objectively for what it is, question it, acknowledge it, love or hate it, and if necessary, detach yourself from it if you want to move forward

C. Being able to assess where it really came from

D. Being able to apply the appropriate little voice mastery technique to reprogram it

Do this consistently, so that you become used to taking control of your own thoughts and actions.

A while back, I was talking to the vice president of sales for a large insurance provider in Alaska, whose sales territory encompasses most of the Pacific Northwest. I asked him what he felt was the most important component in being a great salesperson, manager, or professional. He said that in his nearly twenty years of experience, he had found that "the people who make the best professionals are the people who are the most introspective about their actions and motivations."

When I asked what he meant, he explained, "People who are willing to look inside and question themselves, to question their motives, to question where they're coming from, to assess where they are, and even to challenge their long held assumptions, they're the people who have the ability to move on to greatness."

I totally agree.

Others may dismiss such people as simply "over-thinking" a situation, as being too serious, or taking things too personally, but great leaders are able to make meaningful change to themselves in order to assume bigger roles. As a result, they have a higher propensity to take action. This puts them in positions that require them to make big decisions. And even though they may often make mistakes along the way, that's how they learn, and that's how they get to where they want to be.

By being willing to look inside and question your own thoughts, you also become personally accountable and responsible for your thinking. This gives you a tremendous amount of power. You can then actually prevent yourself from experiencing such debilitating thoughts as denial, blame, justification, or ignorance. You not only become 100 percent responsible for you and your results, but also for the world around you.

Remember that the road to financial development is paved through personal development

This strategy has been a mantra for me for many years and also for several of my closest friends. While others got tired of working on themselves, we never gave up. To this day, I spend hundreds of thousands of dollars, along with countless hours, working on improving myself so that I can serve others better, more clearly, and with more strength. It has translated into incredible financial wealth, extraordinary relationships, and the ability to touch millions of people.

<u>Responsibility</u>
... being personally accountable

Justification
Lay Blame
Denial

(There is no room for these if you are really Responsible.)

Yet for most people (myself included), the little voice does its best to protect a fragile ego. That's why you blame, justify, and make excuses. It's protection. It's autopilot responding. It served you at some point in your life, but also put a cap on your ability to grow. Therefore, the easiest way to manage the little voice when it starts to do this is to simply say, "STOP!" Interrupt it. Stop it. Redirect it. If you have to, smack yourself in the forehead three times.

And then say to yourself (aloud or silently), "I'm blaming again. Stop blaming. Own it!" Remember that if you really look at the word "blame," you'll see that it actually reads "B(e)-LAME"! That should motivate you to stop.

> *Those people who were the top producers, the best leaders, the best managers, were the most introspective.*

Have you ever asked yourself: "Am I doing the right thing? Why am I doing this? Why am I pushing these people so hard? Is this the right thing to do? Is this the right time to be doing this?"

Does this sound familiar? It should. Every great business owner, leader, or parent that I have ever encountered has had a natural tendency to question him or herself. They've been able to step outside of themselves to address and manage the little voice inside.

Yet it's one thing to be introspective and another to over-analyze and wallow in the mire of indecisiveness. That's your little voice stuck in the swamp. Therefore, there is a second key to their greatness:

> *In the face of doubt ... take action anyway!*

Sure, fear comes up. Sure, you doubt yourself. Sure, you question yourself. But there comes a time when you have to have enough little voice control to override the questions and simply take action anyway. Without movement, there is only theory and speculation—no ability to experiment, test, and correct.

Yet, not everybody chooses that path. Many simply go into "unconscious mode," complaining about how they have no control, how they are simply victims of what is happening around them. Never once do they ask themselves, "Is this the right thing to do? What is the value of taking on this challenge? Why am I so afraid? What would be the benefit of going for it?"

In business this can mean the difference between playing a big game or a very small one. If you choose to think like the average employee, you will see yourself as being at the mercy of your boss, the economy ... everything. You merely live a life in which you do as you're told. At that point, you surrender your power and truly become a victim.

Leaders, however, are more introspective. They question themselves, manage their little voice, observe objectively, evaluate, then act and correct, then act and correct again rather than allowing themselves to go on autopilot.

You can choose your thoughts and redirect the ones that you don't want. In my first, (and at the time most profound) personal development course called "Money and You" created by Marshall Thurber, we used to read the words of an old Native American chief by the name of Rolling Thunder who gave a great formula for obtaining control of your own mind. He said (with my thoughts in parentheses):

People have to be responsible for their thoughts, so they have to learn to control them. It may not be easy, but it can be done. First of all, if we don't want to think certain things, we don't say them. (Don't allow yourself to say negative things that reinforce negative thoughts!) We don't have to eat everything we see, and we don't have to say everything we think. (Imagine that!) So we begin by watching our words and speaking with good purpose only. There are times when we must have clear and pure minds with no unwanted thoughts and we have to train and prepare steadily for those times until we are ready. (Training for your ultimate calling!) We don't have to say or think what we don't wish to. We have a choice in those things and we have to realize that and practice using that choice. There is no use condemning yourself for the thoughts and ideas and dreams that come into your mind; so there's no use arguing with yourself or fighting your thoughts. If they keep coming into your head, just let them alone and say, "I don't choose to have such thoughts," and they will soon go away.

If you keep a steady determination and stick with that purpose, you will know how to use that choice and control your consciousness so unwanted thoughts don't come to you anymore. Then you can experience purification completely and in the right way and no impurities can exist in your mind or body any time.

—From *Rolling Thunder* by Doug Boyd (Random House, 1974)

Most people are so used to letting the "CD" play in their minds that they don't even recognize it's playing. They can't see what's happening inside their own heads.

You must be able to look back at moments in your life, whether they were disturbing, successful, or challenging, and assess your own role in them. What did you learn? What part did you cause? Where did your thoughts, actions, and results REALLY come from? Whether you are able to do it in the moment, or months or years later, it is a great step forward. If you can improve your ability to question, evaluate, acknowledge, and even redirect your own little voice, your life will take on richer meaning. The results that you seek will accelerate. And you will be in control of your life. That is called "little voice management."

Self-Value vs. Resistance: Overcoming the Procrastination of Your Dreams

How many times have you put off doing something that you really wanted to do? Write a book? Start a business? Take a group of kids on a cultural trek? There's a reason you put it off and never seem to get to it.

And the good news is that there is a cure! It's probably one of the most powerful little voice mastery techniques that I've worked with, and its applications are nearly universal, whether it's in the realm of sales, relationships, or building personal wealth. It has to do with your ability to clearly *assess value*. I don't just mean the value of a product, service, or opportunity, but more importantly the ability to appropriately assess your own value.

Let's start with confidence. Those people who are the most successful are usually those who have the highest levels of confidence. So where does this confidence come from?

Confidence abounds when your little voice makes you feel good about yourself. It comes from self-assurance that even if you make a mistake, you know you're doing the best you can and that you'll learn and rebound. Confidence comes from knowing there's something good and unique about you, that you have a gift to give and experiences to leverage into opportunities.

However, the problem arises at the moment you choose to expand beyond your current comfort zone, to take that next step in raising your game. It can rear its ugly head whether you're attempting to build a business, nurture a new relationship, improve your health, or expand your portfolio. You meet with internal resistance. And that's why you just never seem to get around to doing it. Know what I mean?

Let's handle this problem so you can get on with your life and fulfill the vision that you have always had for yourself, but haven't gotten around to fulfilling yet.

First, what causes this resistance?

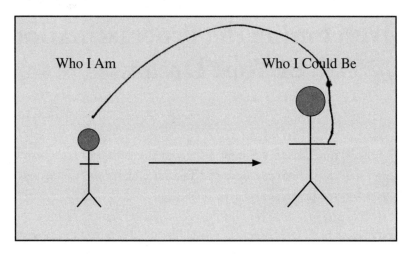

Think of the person you think you are today. If you are like most of us, you would hope there's a bigger, better, more capable person inside! In my travels around the world, having worked with thousands of people, I can tell you that's a pretty common view. You have a great vision of who you could be and what you could have.

When you were a kid, your own picture of yourself was probably huge. I remember, as a kid growing up on a farm in northeastern Ohio, running through the fields with no particular agenda on my mind.

I remember being a rambunctious six-year-old blowing off steam, enjoying the sun, the sky, and the fresh earth under my feet. I particularly remember one day hurtling over row after row of picked corn stalks, thinking that I could either become president of the United States or the first person on the moon! I am sure that you had similar aspirations—sports star, actor, dancer, millionaire, superhero, and so forth.

Yet, as you get older, that vision dims as life's experiences, frustrations, and realities begin to intrude on our dreams. Soon you become programmed to "settle" for less and to be content with random moments of happiness.

I'm going to be a bit spiritual in this chapter because I've always believed that we all have greatness inside of us. I've seen stay-at-home moms who have turned small ideas into multimillion-dollar businesses. We've seen whole IT industries emerge from garages. We've seen thousands of children rescued from disease and hunger and anonymous individuals who give honor and respect to the elderly in hospice care. Every day, men and women take on projects, missions, and causes that change the lives of thousands.

These are not necessarily people you would ever see on the cover of *Time* magazine, or even find much about in a Google search. But somehow they emerge from the masses as great teachers, parents, role models, volunteers, or innovators. Sometimes it's that person whose obesity was so severe, he or she was given only a couple of years to live, and then they went on to shed those pounds to live a long, healthy life. That's greatness!

There's greatness inside of everybody. Whether it's tapped in this lifetime or not depends on your little voice. You may acknowledge that there's greatness inside of you, and as a result, if you are like me, you may also have this nagging little voice that says, "You know, you really ought to get on and do something!"

Perhaps you've always wanted to write a book. It's been inside you for years and you know you should write it. But, for whatever reason, you don't. You may talk about it a lot, but you never take action. Or maybe there's a business you've always wanted to build, an ideal weight you've wanted to reach, a dream house you want to build, or even a trek you want to take. But you don't get to it. *Why?*

There is something between who you are today and who you think you could be—there's something in the middle that keeps you from going there. It's called *resistance.*

It comes from many different things. It's one of the most devastating little voices inside each of our minds, and I'm sure you recognize it. It sounds a little like this: "Well, what makes you think that book would be any good anyway? What makes you think you can write it?"

If you aren't careful, you end up going through a systematic process of devaluing yourself and your project, until your energy is sufficiently low enough to NOT take action, and you procrastinate one more time. You never get around to writing the book, starting the business, or conquering the mountain.

Life gets in the way. In fact, cleaning the garage, spending a few more hours at work, running a couple more errands, or answering some more e-mails all of a sudden becomes more important than the dream that simmers inside of you.

(By the way, this is a great example because it just now took me the better part of a day and a half to sit down and continue this chapter! I had e-mails to answer, partners to talk to, errands to run, an office to un-clutter ... see what I mean?)

We all feel like we *could* be great, but when it comes down to sitting in front of the computer right now, putting my fingers to the keyboard and writing, a little voice says, "You don't have anything worthwhile to talk about! Who would want to hear about this? Who cares about the little voice, anyway? This is a stupid idea. Who else would want to know about this? Besides, how are you going to sell it? Have you thought about distribution?" And so on, and so on.

If I demean it in my own brain, I will end up giving it less value. If that happens, I'll end up walking away from the keyboard, which only justifies my inability to get to the task and causes me to say to myself, "Obviously I'm not inspired enough to do this right now. I'll do it later." The resistance now takes the form of procrastination!

The real resistance is self-induced.
If your own perceived value is diminished, you aren't motivated
enough to try to overcome the resistance.

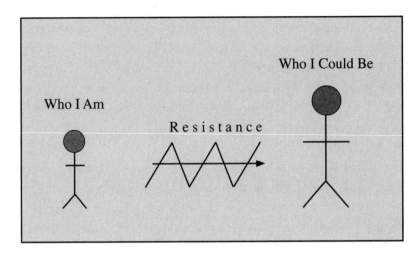

The resistance can take the form of the little voice saying things like, "Not good enough! Not capable enough! You don't know what you're talking about!"

A few months ago, I conducted a program that I had dreaded preparing for. A crowd of people was coming to spend four days learning from me, and I had no idea what I was going to talk to them about! My little voice was saying, "They've already been to a bunch of my other programs. They've heard me before. I can't tell them anything new. I have nothing to offer."

I was blocked because I was listening to my own negative little voice and believing it. And because my brain was blocked, I created all kinds of stress for myself. Finally, the breakthrough occurred when I was able to shut my little voice up and realize I was creating my *own resistance*.

This was obviously the message I was meant to deliver. So when I opened that program, I said, "The reason people have writer's block, never write the play they could write, never enter the Tour de France, or never amass a portfolio of valuable real estate is because they have *resistance* to doing it. Where does the resistance come from? It comes from the value (or lack of value) that you place on yourself and your own dream! The resistance comes in many forms. It often sounds like this: I gotta clean the house. I gotta do some filing. I gotta make some phone calls.'"

That became the theme for the next four days because all of us experience it. It also became the motivation for writing this book. That the gift you have to give— the book, the play, the business, the life that you want—is only seconds away. Many will go an entire lifetime and never touch it. But if you can begin to build the confidence, the energy, and mostly realize the value of YOU—you will touch that greatness many times in your life.

There always seems to be something that mysteriously appears between you and your dreams. The reason for that is that whatever gets in the way—whether it's cleaning your closets or making some phone calls—has more value to you in that immediate moment than the book you want to write. Think about that for a second. Getting all those phone calls made has more immediate value to you than the value of a book that could potentially touch the lives of thousands of people. How ludicrous is that?

How many things are you allowing to get in *your* way, forming resistance that stops you from being who you're supposed to be? Because essentially, at some level, what the little voice is saying is that the phone calls or the closet cleaning are more important than sitting down to write your book, more important than being *who you are supposed to be.*

When you *really* look at procrastination, the first toll that little voice takes is on your *confidence.* As a matter of fact, I've worked with thousands of people over the years in both sales and leadership, and the issue of effectiveness many times boils down to confidence.

The more times you allow that little voice to procrastinate and justify not doing something, the less confident you become in taking on the bigger tasks that you should be accomplishing.

> *If your confidence is low, then your resistance will be high, and you will never accomplish the things you set out to do or become who you want to be!*

I've seen so many people fail to achieve their full potential because they were too busy sorting through piles of resistance. A woman came up to me in one of my workshops and said, "I've had this idea about a book for a long time." I asked her why she hadn't written it yet, and she said, "Well, I've had a lot of great ideas, but I just never seem to get around to it."

I asked her, "So what's it going to take for you to do it? Are you going to schedule some time? Develop a list of priorities?"

That the gift you have to give— the book, the play, the business, the life that you want is only seconds away.

None of that seemed to work for her, until we began to discuss the concept of self-value. I put up a flip-chart (see previous resistance diagram) and said, "Resistance often comes from people undervaluing themselves. When you do that, you're devaluing the natural gift that you have to give, the one you were put on this planet to share. And because of that, *everything else* becomes more important, which is why you don't get to it. That's why you end up frustrated."

That was when the truth hit home for her. Within four months, her book was complete.

If there is frustration about not having fulfilled your potential by now, imagine the frustration you'll feel somewhere down the road when you're fifty, sixty, seventy, or eighty years old, as you think to yourself, "How come I didn't do it? Why didn't I do it? I should have done it. It's too late now and I can't do it." (By the way, it's never too late.)

That frustration is born in the battle between all the little voices in your head.

Between the self-deprecating "I'm-not-important-enough" little voice and the part of you that really wants to accomplish something you're meant to do, you'll find frustration. You see, there is a part of you that knows you're bound for something wonderful that won't completely die, because it comes from a deeper place inside of you.

But it gets tired from the battle that it's continually fighting with your resistance—with the other little voice that says, "We gotta deal with what's more important at the moment. We'll get to that later." So as a result, that part of you begins to place more value on what's right in front of your face than what's down the road.

Think about this:

You wouldn't be able to see the future if you were not meant to create it!!

That's right. You CAN see the future. You have had glimpses of it from time to time. Where do you think that comes from? And how do you think the future gets created? It's you!!

You have always had the ability to create it. You were born with it. That's why you get so tired, frustrated, and even cynical over time if you keep letting others create your future for you!!

Joe Zemaitis is my son's swimming and running coach, and he's an incredible young man. He's also a world-class professional triathlete, runs several large swim teams, and speaks to youngsters all over the world about how to become the best they can be. He also coached the first eight-year-old to set the record for being the youngest person to ever swim from Alcatraz to San Francisco. Following constant urging and coaching from me and others, Joe has written a great book called *Joe's Rules*. It's about developing the greatness in every child through sports, whether your child is naturally athletic or not.

One of these rules is posted above his bed:

"Most people fail rather than succeed because they give up what they really want for what they want at the moment."

When it's 4:00 in the morning and he has to get up and go for a bike ride, there's a part of him that would rather stay in bed. But if that little voice wins and staying in bed holds more value, he will never win the next triathlon.

One of his other motivational rules is also posted in strategic locations throughout his house:

"Somewhere else in the world, someone is practicing while you're not, and when you meet him, he'll beat you."

By putting yourself in a routine of practicing, you automatically program your mind to place a higher value on the end goal, whatever that is: to win a triathlon, to write a book, to lose weight, to amass wealth, to build a business, to have a great relationship, or to improve the quality of life for your family.

Repetition builds conditioning. By repeatedly putting in too many hours at the office, having too many phone calls to make, partying with your friends rather than spending that time at home or with your significant other, you're conditioning resistance toward building a better relationship. How does that happen? The more times you repeat the scenario of hanging out with your friends and having another drink at the bar, the more value you place on that in-the-moment experience. It becomes more valuable to you at that moment than developing the loving relationship with your family that you may really want more in the long run. You are actually conditioning yourself to place greater value on those other things instead of on your own dreams.

The reason your dreams get obstructed, is because "cleaning your closets" or "making phone calls"—are given more value in that immediate moment than your dreams

Those things that are standing in front of you are awfully tempting, but you've allowed the value of that moment to override the long-term value of a future moment. Why? Because you've let the little voice convince you, "You deserve this right now, and that will come later, and besides...you're probably not able to pull that off anyway."

Let me put it another way. Fred, the founder of several successful weight loss companies in America, told a great story that relates to this. Early in the development of his weight loss businesses, he had a woman who was suffering from severe health problems related to her obesity. He attempted to sell her on a weight loss program that included a very simple routine of proper nutrition, exercise, and a healthier lifestyle. It was obvious even to a layman that this woman's life would be in danger if she did not do something!

Yet, she claimed she could not afford the $450 per month for the program. She said it was "too expensive." With a sigh, Fred looked at her, then looked out the window and directed the woman's attention to a shiny, hot-looking Mercedes convertible parked right outside.

Fred asked her, "Would you like to have that car?" The woman smiled widely and said, "Of course, but ..."

Fred cut her off. He went on to ask her how much she thought that car was worth. She guessed about $80–90,000. He told her that was pretty close. Then he said, "If I told you that you could have that very car for $6,000, would you buy it?" She laughed and said, "In a heartbeat!" A seriousness came over his face as he looked her square in the eye and said, "You would pay $6,000 to drive off in that hot Mercedes right now, but wouldn't pay $450 to get your life back. Is that what you are telling me?"

Needless to say, the woman bought the program and got herself back in shape, and Fred has gone on to build great wealth for himself and his businesses. What Fred knew all too well was that most people assess themselves and their future as being less valuable than the things they can have in the present moment. Immediate gratification makes you feel good about yourself *now*.

Imagine that I put a bag with $10,000 cash in it in front of you right now and say that you could either have that money right now, or I'd give you $15,000 cash in six months if you work out five days a week for one hour a day and go on a reasonably healthy diet. Which would you do? That $10K is tempting, and most would go for the easy and immediate cash rather than making more money and being healthy. Why?

If your self-esteem is low, you're going to do whatever it takes to make you feel good in the moment. That's how blocks and resistance are created. It would be tough for me, too. I might even go for the ten grand. Why? Because it would make me feel good *right now*. But if I felt really good about me, I'd say, "No, I'm going to go for the $15,000 because I'd rather have ten years added my life." It takes a person with high self-esteem to do that.

That doesn't mean that if you don't have great self-esteem, you're all screwed up. It just means, as I said in the last chapter, that if you have developed the ability to step outside yourself, view yourself objectively and say, "Whoa! I'm devaluing me! That's what's causing the resistance!" you're starting to win the game. You're managing the little voice.

I would recommend you sit down and make a list of who you imagine yourself to be five or ten years from now. In an ideal scene and an ideal environment, who would you be?

- *What do you want to be?*
- *What do you want to have?*
- *What do you want to accomplish?*
- *What is it that you want to create?*

What are your answers? Make a list now. Write it all down. What's your little voice saying while you are writing the list?

Notice all the little voice chatter that comes up while you are writing or thinking about it.

Notice how that chatter justifies why you're not working on those things you really want. Stuff like: "I don't have time," "I'll work on it later," or "I'm just dreaming." Chances are, you'll find a common little voice theme that is devaluing your own power. So make another list of what the little voice's responses are.

That's right. Write them down. Notice how much power they have or don't have. Interesting, eh?

You have a great gift to give. As someone once said, "Greed is having a gift, and not giving it." By not being who you are supposed to be, you are not only ripping yourself off, but you are letting "stuff" prevent you from allowing your talents, gifts, and dreams to benefit everyone else. Technically, you're betraying them, too!

Each of the more than six billion of us on this planet has something to offer. We don't all have to cure cancer or save the planet or create a multimillion-dollar business. But we all have something to offer, some gift. And it's our job to figure it out and use it in our lifetime. That knowledge drives me. I also think it would drive you if you were able to step outside yourself and look at it. But if you devalue yourself and believe you're not worthy or capable, you'll create all kinds of resistance.

These days, particularly in the West and in developed economies, we all get so much for so little. We have fewer worries about putting food on the table, finding shelter, or securing health care. We have governments, schools, families. So much is provided for us that we take these things for granted. And I think that over the last twenty or thirty years, our ability to properly assess value has been distorted.

That's why for those who are in sales, the biggest obstacle is people's objections to price. People compare prices and opt for the cheapest item, rather than assessing true value, because they assume value to be equal. That's because they are used to getting so much for basically nothing. There is so much that we haven't ever had to work for, and equally as much that we haven't had to pay for. In each generation, this attitude seems to become more widespread.

Think of how much your kids have now, compared to what you had when you were their age. Because of this, we have lost the ability to assess value properly. That's why the number one objection in sales is price. But it isn't really about price ... it's about value.

For most of our great-grandparents, this wasn't really the case. There was a time when if something had value, people would work their tails off to have it, no matter the expense. My great-grandfather didn't have two pennies to pinch together, but because he wanted to come to America, he found a way to do it. He didn't let his little voice say that it was too expensive. He valued his family and his freedom so much that he wanted to leave Eastern Europe so he could have a better life for his family. He sacrificed everything. When he finally got to America, he threw a pack on his back and literally sold rags in the streets of New York in order to make enough money to bring the rest of his family to America.

Would you ever see this today? You see it in those who risk their lives to cross the southern borders of the U.S. in order to earn money to feed their families. But for many with less impoverished lifestyles, assessing value properly is becoming a lost art. And that's why there's so much focus on price. (If you work in sales, fear not! There's a way to overcome the price issue very quickly. Go to www.salesdogs. com for more information.)

The most catastrophic outcome of this is not only in the lost ability to assess the value of products, services, and commodities, but in the loss of the ability to assess your own value. You see the young founders of YouTube make billions. You see *American Idol* winners splashed across magazine covers. And you forget that those are anomalies and *not the norm.* Left unchecked, it can distort your perception of your own worth and minimize the value of all those everyday people who have built great businesses, made good money, and nurtured great families and relationships. They did it one day at a time, one step at a time, and so can you.

The danger in all of this is that you learn to underestimate your own value! To anybody who picks up this book, please remember one thing:

There's a very special person inside of you.
You have an important gift to share.

And if you challenge the little voice on a daily basis, you will come to finally believe that you really do have enormous value.

Then you will complete the book, build the business, support the relationship, and make yourself into the person you are meant to be. And you'll never have to compare yourself to another human being and find yourself lacking in comparison.

I've been teaching personal development programs for over twenty-five years, and I'll tell you what happens for most people sitting in a seminar room. They see a person in front of the room talking about building wealth, personal actualization, or whatever, and they immediately make excuses and justifications for not having achieved the things they wanted to achieve themselves—for not being the bigger, better people they were supposed to be. The most common little voice excuse is: "That's great, but my situation is DIFFERENT!" Heard that one before?

One young fellow from New Zealand attended one of my courses, and when I asked him how he felt the course was going, he said, "You know, as I sit here and listen to you and to others in front of the room, I really believe that you guys have been successful. I know that it's real, you've done it."

Sensing there was something else he wanted to say, I pressed him to continue. He said, "I look around the room at all these other people, and I suspect they're probably going to be able to follow your process and become successful, too."

So I asked where he was going with this. And he continued, "Well, my situation's different. Because of what I have to deal with, I'm not sure that I could do that."

In all my years of teaching, coaching, mentoring, and running businesses, I can tell you that for the majority of people, that's one of the most common and nastiest little voices of all! That's why fewer than 5 percent of people in any given program actually go out and do something with it. It's because of self-doubt and a low perceived value of one's self covered over by excuses and justification in the form of the phrase: "My situation's different!"

Look, your situation is NOT different! Is your situation different because of family? Heartbreak? Financial calamity? Bad experience? Disappointment? Personal skeletons in the closet? How did I know all those things? Hmmmm. It's because we ALL have them. It's just your little voice justifying the lack of results by convincing you that you are specifically handicapped.

It's a LIE! It's only your little voice creating resistance!!!!!

That's why my sole purpose, in most all the work that I do, is to get people to see their own value. I can see value in people, and most people can see it in others, too. But, we have a hard time seeing it in ourselves. For whatever reason, the little voice has been programmed that way. Maybe it's for self-preservation, survival, or protection from disappointment. The reason doesn't really matter.

My job, your job, and the job of any leader, parent, friend, or coach is to find the strength in others, reach inside, pull it out, and help them actually see it for themselves.

> *Once you can get a glimpse of your own brilliance,*
> *you instantly rehabilitate your sense of self-value.*

Then you'll go out and write the book you need to write, lose the weight you want to lose, amass the wealth you want, or solidify the relationships that are important to you.

But only when you get your little voice to understand the value of *you* can all the resistant garbage drop. The resistance is only *you* believing that you're not worthy, that you don't have enough to offer, or that nobody will want to listen or hear from you anyway!

So when you look at the person you are today and where you want to be, there is a gap. And nature hates a void. Something will fill in that gap. What is it? Spaces to clean, closets to organize, phone calls to make, errands to run, or extra hours to sleep in. The reason we fill the void with menial tasks is because those trivial things seem more important at the moment than we do. It's just your mind playing tricks on you.

> *Nothing is more important than you delivering your gift,*
> *your talent, to your family, your friends, your community, or your job.*
> *Nothing is more important than that.*

That's why you were put here—to do something!
Not just to occupy space.

To be able to solve a problem for somebody.
To make somebody's life a little bit better.

Look at the evidence! If we were meant to be alone, God, the Great Spirit, or the cosmos (whatever beliefs you subscribe to) wouldn't have put more than six billion of us on the planet. We are obviously *supposed* to coexist and support each other. Yet if we all doubt ourselves and place higher value on other people than on ourselves, everyone ends up waiting for someone else to do it.

The select few who actually do something are the ones who emerge as leaders. Some of them are good and some are bad. But they're the ones who believe they've got something to give and they're going to get their butts out of bed at 4:00 a.m. to do something about it. They perceive that what they've got to offer has more value than lying in bed. They value their gifts. They value themselves. They value their missions and themselves as emissaries of those missions. Sometimes it's a conscious choice on their part, and sometimes it's not. But the results are real.

I maintain that everyone who picks up this book is a leader, because otherwise you wouldn't have picked it up. There's a part of you, some small part of your psyche, that grabbed this book because you know there's something bigger and better inside you. I fully believe that.

Buckminster Fuller once talked about the difference between "making a living" and doing what you are meant to do. He said, "The bumblebee does not have to 'earn a living.' It simply does what it is supposed to do. It does 'what is spontaneously arousable' in it to do."

What if we lived in a world where everybody did
what they were supposed to do because they loved doing it?
What kind of a world would that be?

Simply do what is spontaneously arousable in you to do. What is naturally exciting, what you are naturally curious about, what you would do for free because you love it. (After the vacations and recreational activities!)

It would be amazing. And that's why many of the businesses that our SalesPartners franchise owners work with get such great results in such a short time. Because all of our processes are designed to bring out those natural strengths, abilities, and talents in others.

The only thing filling the gap between the "big you" and the "little you" is your own perceived value of yourself. It's either resistance or it's an accelerator. It depends on your little voice.

Confidence:
Resurrecting the Hero
Inside of You

B y practicing little voice mastery techniques, you gain the ability to permanently boost your confidence.

What I always say in sales and communication is that, yes, it's important to have good technique, but it's more important to have *confidence*. You need to be aligned with your message—in other words, walking the talk. All the parts that go into representing yourself to others have to be congruent with each other; they have to be compatible and harmonious.

If you want to be a personal trainer and you're forty pounds overweight with a cigarette hanging out of your mouth, you're not congruent with your message. Congruency means that you're firing on all cylinders. Your brain, your mind, your body, your emotions, your spirituality—they're all lined up and in agreement.

There's nothing worse than you representing something that in your own heart you don't believe in. If you're telling somebody, "I'm really confident this is going to work!" and you're really *not* confident about it at all, it will show through in your tone and demeanor. It's going to affect your actions. You may be saying the words, but without confidence it's very, very difficult to get your point across convincingly.

> *That's why one of the most important sales of all, in any part of your life, is selling you to you!*

And that's where confidence comes from. When you're convinced that you know what you're talking about, that you have *earned* the right to talk about something, that you have the credibility, or that you are passionate enough about what you're talking about, then that tone, that confidence, gets communicated to whomever you're communicating with. That, in turn, instills confidence in them. So confidence, or a lack of confidence, is conveyed almost immediately, and usually subconsciously, to anyone you talk to. You've probably had the experience of talking to someone who seemed to be saying the right words, but all the while you're thinking to yourself, "Something's not quite right. It doesn't feel to me like this person knows what he or she is talking about." The reason you may be thinking that is because that other person may not have confidence in their *own* credibility.

In Sydney, Australia, I met a guy who was a truck driver. He came to our program because he knew he could be doing more with his life. When the workshop was over, he promptly went out and raised over $30 million for his first real estate development! Laz is now a multimillionaire who is fully accustomed to thinking big...the way *his* spirit is supposed to think. The only thing that happened at that workshop was that he got a brief glimpse of who he could really be. With that glimpse, his confidence soared and the resistance dropped.

He later told me that he has been unable to do some of the things he used to do. He said, "I can't go back to thinking small. It's not in me anymore!"

A lot of this goes back to our discussion in the last chapter about self-value. The bottom line is, if you don't value yourself, you won't have the confidence to play a much bigger game.

So then, the question is, how do you get confidence? The answer to that is actually a lot simpler than you would think. Once you learn how to get confidence, you now have the ability to prevent yourself from talking yourself out of stuff. And how do you do that? The easiest way is through repetition.

> ***If you repeat something often enough, your confidence will naturally build because repetition creates experience.***

If you look at the age-old example of learning to ride your bike when you were a child, you may remember how unsteady and nervous you were. Think of when you tried to teach your own child. Some kids take to it straight away, but others need more practice. And the more practice they get, the more confident they become. It's the same thing for you whenever you're trying something new.

Lack of confidence comes from a fear of the unknown or a fear of not having accomplished something. In other words, I'm not going to have a lot of confidence in my sales ability if I've never sold anything. The more things I sell, the more confidence I have in my ability to sell. But then again, let's say I take on a new product, or I have a new boss. And while I had confidence dealing with my old boss because I dealt with him so often, now I have a new boss and I'm nervous. I have butterflies, and I lack the confidence to deal with him because I just haven't had the experience. So the lack of confidence is the result of a lack of experience. Obviously, the way to gain confidence, then, is through repetition and lots of experience.

How do you do that? By putting yourself on the firing line—a lot! If you need to have more confidence in learning how to swim, negotiating, or building a business, then you need to go out there and *do* more of it.

By the same token, the other way of gaining confidence through **repetition** is by practicing, drilling, and role-playing. In *SalesDogs*, we talk about practicing objections and elevator pitches, and doing them over and over again until after a while you've done it *so many times* it's no big deal. Then, you can do it for real in public with ease. It's almost a reflex at that point. Your confidence appears naturally. It's simple, but you have to practice.

The problem with most people who lack confidence is that they allow their little voices to go into overdrive and bombard them with thoughts like, "You don't know what you're talking about! You don't know what you're doing! It's not your thing! You've never been able to do anything like this before. What makes you think you can get away with it now?" Repetition through practice and drilling will get that little voice to *shut up*.

Another way to build confidence is to simply shut up *all* the little voices that are telling you that you can't do something. Each time you *stop* the little voice, ask yourself, "Is this something I can learn? Is this something I can gain more confidence in with more repetition?" Doing this will help you to obtain confidence.

But there is still one other very important way of gaining confidence. This is called **immersion.** You hear this a lot with regard to learning a language, but the principle is the same for pretty much anything. Immersion means to bury yourself in whatever skill you're attempting to master. If you want to learn to speak Spanish, you go to Mexico and you're forced to learn it just to get through the day. If you want to learn to make sales calls, you make heaps of sales calls.

> *Get yourself in as deep and as quickly as you possibly can. You may not succeed, but you will have obtained a ton of experience.*

Or you could swim fifty-plus laps to increase your lap speed, or hit hundreds of golf balls to improve your stroke.

By having so much activity going on, you're simply too busy to even be aware of fear and lack of confidence, and they're forced out of your brain. In other words, if you put yourself in a pressure-cooker situation, in which you're bombarded with the experience, you just don't have time to argue with yourself. You're just surviving. And your confidence (or lack of it) doesn't even enter the equation.

For example, you're at the top of a steep mountain with skis clipped to your boots. Your confidence is waning. Yet, once you *start* going down the slope, it doesn't matter whether you have confidence or not. Your immediate concern is just staying alive. But, once you've made it, you feel great because you did it. You then have more confidence to try it again. The next time you try the same downhill run, it won't be nearly as difficult.

> ### *Confidence is something you worry about before you take on a task ... not as much when you are in it.*

It's about being resourceful and figuring out a way down that mountain, because otherwise you're going to get hurt. It's the same in business. If you're already in a negotiation, you don't have time to worry about whether you're confident or credible. You just have to get through it. You have to be resourceful and do what you have to do.

Get yourself in as deep and as quickly as you possibly can. You may not succeed, but you will have obtained a ton of experience. And the pressure of getting through the situation will squeeze the doubting little voice from your brain because you'll be so focused on the task at hand. You'll no longer have time to worry because you have to be more attuned, more adept. Naturally, your sense of mental acuity has to be higher, and out of necessity, the lack of confidence just automatically goes away.

Confidence builds through the experience.

There is another way to artificially infuse your mind with confidence. You're going to think this is nuts, but it works. It's a little voice mastery technique we call **bragging,** or boasting. Believe it or not, this is a real, physical exercise that works. Here's how you do it.

Recall a time in your life where you've had some success. Then go up to a mirror, or to another person (preferably someone who knows what you're doing), and talk about how great you were/are in that situation and about the great things that you did. Even if they're not entirely true, it doesn't matter. This is a drill. As a matter of fact, in this drill it's okay to lie a little! Stand on a table, beat your chest, pump your fists ... do whatever it takes physically to put yourself into a state that exudes great confidence.

It's only a game that you are playing with your head. If you do this loudly and profoundly in an animated fashion for about thirty seconds, you will feel an adrenalin rush. For that moment, your confidence about anything will soar. You need to know what it *feels* like to be great—to be the best.

Your little voice is probably already saying, "That's a ridiculous idea. You'll look stupid. And what's this got to do with anything, anyway?" One of my mentors once said that THAT little voice is the "murderer" inside you. And the mere fact that it even pops up tells you that you need to do this exercise.

The final way to access confidence is an exercise we teach in our seminars called **modeling.** Modeling means mimicking or physically, mentally, and emotionally acting like someone else. You simply model someone else who has confidence! In our programs, we have people model short video clips of people like John F. Kennedy, Martin Luther King, Jr., Gandhi, Eddie Murphy, or even Henry V. It can be anybody who's demonstrated supreme confidence, boldness, or bravery. Find your own role models and model them—their speech, their actions, and their way of thinking.

Ask yourself things like, "If I were Henry V right now, what would I do? What would I say? How would I act?" By putting yourself in that person's place, you artificially, at least for the moment, own their confidence. Ultimately, with persistence and repetition, your own feelings will begin to match those of that other person who actually has the confidence.

And then, lo and behold, because you've actually taken yourself through the experience and felt the confidence, your own confidence builds.

But you know what else about modeling? It's a trick because all along, it's been *your* confidence! Even though you are modeling someone else, that confidence comes from YOU! It's a way to use someone else's power to bring out the best in you.

There is an old children's story about a young man who lived long, long ago (when all the best stories happened). He was bending over a small pond looking for fish when he caught a glimpse of his own reflection. He recoiled from what he saw. He couldn't believe how ugly his image was. He was deeply ashamed and sought the help of the local fairy godmother, as do most troubled young men! However, she was only able to help him in a limited way. She gave him a mask to wear which looked just like a real human face. It of course came with a warning that he could never take it off or look in the mirror. But this mask face was wonderfully handsome, and when the young man put the mask on, there was no way of knowing that the mask was not his real face. For many years, the young man wore the mask and people from all across the land would comment on how handsome he was and what a grand character he had.

The time came, of course, when he met the girl of his dreams and he wanted to ask her to marry him, but he didn't want the dark secret of his mask to stand between them. After much thinking and soul-searching, he decided that he would tell her about the mask. When the time came and he shared his secret, he warned her that she would be horrified by his real face. Hesitantly, he removed the mask that he had been hiding behind for so long. When he took it off, she gasped and said, "Why, you're just the same!" He had become what he had pretended to be for so long.

And that's the way it is with confidence. If you wear it, practice it, model it, and repeat it again and again, you will become it.

So, confidence is not necessarily about your abilities or past experiences. It's about believing in yourself, and having confidence in *you*. You have to trust yourself. Even though you may not know much about something—like negotiating a sale or getting through a delicate situation with your spouse—you still trust yourself enough to go ahead with it anyway, because you know you'll get through it.

You know that, when you look at your track record, you've probably rarely ever really let yourself down. You've always been able to bring yourself through difficult situations. You've made it okay each time. Sometimes you've won. Sometimes you screwed up. But in most cases, you learned something. No matter what, you've managed to bring yourself through it.

The ultimate confidence is trusting yourself and your ability to prevail, even if you have doubt in your ability to pull it off in the moment. You have confidence in knowing you will make *something* happen. You will learn *something*. You can trust yourself to be resourceful. So how do you do that?

One way is to take a look at your history. If you're going into a tough situation, look at what you *have* accomplished. Look at all the instances when you were faced with a situation like this. What happened? What worked? What didn't work? Write it down! Where were your wins? What you'll find in many cases is that you've already built an impressive track record that you didn't even realize you had.

Most people are fairly capable when it comes to life's challenges. Usually, most people have the ability to get things done. The only thing that undermines you is the little voice in your brain that says, "You can't do it. You don't know enough. You don't have enough confidence." And that's nonsense!

If you wear it, practice it, model it, and repeat it again and again, you will become it. That's the way it is with confidence.

You've been training your whole life for whatever it is you're about to do right now. So the best solution is to get into it as quickly as you can because, at the very least, you'll be totally immersed and will be gaining tons of experience through repetition. Plus, once you're in action mode, you will be naturally forced to manipulate the little voice in your brain into believing that you've got enough of "whatever-it-takes" to get through the task before you.

Look at it this way: Except for very few instances, you won't die. You won't get eaten alive, you'll be okay, and at the very least you'll come away having learned something.

With little voice mastery, then, the most important thing when it comes to your mind and your actions being congruent with each other is confidence. If you're in business, negotiating, selling, or attempting to get your point across, a lack of confidence is immediately sensed by other parties. Unfortunately, it can be interpreted as a sign of weakness. As much as I would like to say that it's not a big deal, it is a big deal.

> ***Even the nicest person may take advantage of somebody
> who doesn't have confidence.***

If you're serious about gaining confidence from the inside out, about being true to who you are, and getting a whole lot more from your life, your business, your relationships, and your ability to create wealth or your family life ... get serious about following these steps:

- Don't talk yourself out of things that could be good for you! Just because something's uncomfortable doesn't necessarily mean it's not good for you!

- Repeat the experiences that you need to have confidence in again and again, in role-playing exercises and for real.

- Practice overcoming the objections that hinder your progress. Practice them in the mirror, with a friend, and in real-life situations.

- Immerse yourself in the project, task, or occasion at hand. Get yourself in as deep and as quickly as you possibly can.

- Model someone you know whom you respect, someone who has the confidence you are looking for.

Follow the steps we've already outlined—even standing on a chair and beating your chest while telling yourself how great you are and bragging to the world at the top of your lungs. You'll see that as your energy grows, so will your confidence. And the person with the highest energy wins!

> **The person**
> **with the**
> **HIGHEST**
> **ENERGY**
> **WINS!**

I once heard someone say, "Confidence? Isn't that what other people have?" Well, not anymore. You can do this. You can be confident. And when you are ... others will have confidence in you.

Authenticity:
Winning by Being Real

When it comes to being really effective in whatever it is you want to do, the people who seem to be the most successful, the most powerful, have the best relationships, and make the most money, are also the people who are the most real.

What I mean is that what you see is what you get. People like this pull very few punches. They're very honest. They have high integrity, meaning that they're true to themselves. They are authentic. Being authentic means that you aren't trying to be like anybody else—not who your mom, your dad, your schoolteachers, preacher, or friends want you to be. You're just really being you.

But if it were that easy, we'd all be super-achievers with fantastic careers, perfect families, full bank accounts, and flawless health. The biggest blockage to being truly genuine and real is when your little voice starts worrying about what other people think of you.

The biggest fear most people have is the fear of looking foolish in front of others.

In a previous chapter, I said that most people's biggest fear is of public humiliation; more people fear this than death, actually. They're afraid of looking stupid in other people's eyes. Most times, it's the only thing that stands between you and authenticity. But when you're really you, which I believe is what most people truly want, you have a chance to access all the God-given strengths that you have inside you, to be who you really are. That's when you're most effective.

The reason little voice mastery is so powerful is because it propels you to realize and experience who you really are. Earlier in the book, I talked about the fact that while your little voices may be yours, they may not all have begun with you. One voice may be that of somebody else telling you what you should do. There could be another voice telling you who you should be or how you should act. For example, some of us still believe that boys are supposed to be tough and assertive, while girls should be sweet and shy. Whose little voice is saying that?

I have a very dear friend who spent several years of her life attempting to get out of a bad relationship. As an example of how bad this relationship was for her, the person she was with was unkind enough to stand her in front of a mirror and tell her how ugly she was every day. He would tell her that she should be grateful to be with him because she was so ugly. And unfortunately, she began to believe it. She became so concerned with pleasing him that she lost herself in the process.

It wasn't until she had done enough little voice mastery on herself that she could understand how much her boyfriend had been manipulating her, which had kept her locked in a terrible place emotionally. Luckily, she obtained the strength to gain control of the little voices—hers and his—and get out of the relationship. Now she's free and happy. And now, she surrounds herself with people who like her for who she is and what her talents are. She's happier than ever, making more money than she ever has before, and she has infinitely more energy than she ever did before, because finally she's given herself permission to be who she really is. (By the way ... she's gorgeous!)

Whether it's getting away from the abuse of others or from the abuse you do to yourself, in order to be effective, you must be who you are. Think about it. If you're entering into some sort of business or personal relationship, would you want a partner who simply puts on a good show, or would you want to deal with someone who is genuine?

For instance, a guy comes to the door selling roofing services. He's got the van out front with all the correct signage. He's noticed that your roof could stand a facelift and he's offering you a good price. He says he can have it done within two weeks, with minimum disruption to you! One part of you thinks, "Great! This guy is just what I want. I don't have to go through the hassle of finding someone else. His price is good and it would really add some value to my home."

But there's a little voice in your head saying, "Why is he shifting from foot to foot? Why can't he maintain eye contact? Why does he stumble over his words? What is he hiding? I'm not going to deal with this guy. He's probably trying to pull one over on me."

He is so nervous that he cannot even be himself. His nervous little voice makes your little voice nervous and there is no deal made.

So you close the door and possibly miss out on a good deal, and Mr. Roofing loses a good paying job. Mr. Roofing needs to get his confidence act together or no one will take him up on his really good offer, no matter how nice a guy he is or how genuine he seems.

The biggest fear a lot of people have is that if they're real, nobody will like them.

Many people think, "If you see me for who I really am, if I show you my vulnerability, if I show you what's really going on, you'll see this cesspool of neuroses in there and you won't like me." Well, the truth is, we all have cesspools of neuroses. That's nothing to be worried about. My experience in all these years is that people *appreciate* other people who are willing to be candid.

Don't get me wrong. Nobody wants to listen to your sob story or your laundry list of problems. But they certainly do want somebody who's going to be honest and real. Because when push comes to shove and challenges arise, they want someone they can trust, someone who will be straight with them. That's why one of the most powerful forms of little voice mastery is to eliminate the fear of what other people think of you. It may be what stands in the way of becoming *who you really are!*

One of my dear friends is a fellow by the name of Kim White; he's also a great advisor and counselor. Any time I've ever had trepidation about doing a big presentation (yes, it's true—even after doing thousands of them, I sometimes still get a nervous, upset stomach), I speak with Kim. *My* little voice can go crazy like everybody else's. It says things to me like, "You don't know what you're talking about! What are you going to do for two and a half hours, or three and a half days? You don't have enough material! They're going to hate you!"

But, what I know is that it's my little voice! And that little voice *can be turned off* or redirected as fast as it got turned on. If I can't deal with it myself, I go to someone I know, someone who knows how to deal with my little voice. As I said early on in the book, Kim is one of those people, and Jayne Johnson and Alan's team are others. I have a few special, very qualified people like that in my life. And when I'm in a situation like that, I say to them, "Look, this is what my little voice is doing right now, and I can't shake it."

These folks are trained to help get me out of it. Kim White said something to me once before a major presentation that I'll never forget; it's helped me get through many tough times. I'm going to repeat it to you because I think it applies to everyone.

He said, "Blair, you have a gift." Now, you may be thinking, "Well, that doesn't sound like such a big deal." Intellectually, each of us knows we all have a gift, but to *know* that emotionally and *believe* it is a big deal. You, reading this book right now, also have a gift. I've said it a thousand times, and I'll say it again:

You have a God-given talent, something you're supposed to do!

Some people will never use that gift. Some people will come close to it. But the people who get really close to being who they are and doing what they're supposed to be doing are the ones who have managed to shut up the distracting little voice; they are authentic.

You know you are close to accessing your special talent or gift when what you are doing not only gives you great joy, but you find that's where you seem to get the most wins ... where time disappears and you're having a blast. That's when you're delivering your gift.

Kim White said, "Blair, you make people feel good about who they are!" and I said, "I do?"

"Yeah, you do," he said. My response was, "I thought I help people sell."

He went on, "You help people to sell. Yeah, you help them build great teams, but really the core of what you do is that you help people feel good about who they are and how big they are!"

> *You know you're close to accessing your special talent when what you're doing not only gives you great joy, but you find that's where you seem to get the most wins ... where time disappears and you're having a blast.*

He explained that we all have problems, we all have issues to deal with, but there's a genius inside of everyone, and that my strength is helping people to see that genius, to bring it out, to work with it, and to leverage it.

My first impulse when someone says that kind of thing to me is to look down at my shoes and say, "Aw shucks, it's no big thing!" It's hard to own that kind of praise. Have you ever felt that way? You get a compliment, and you think what you're being complimented on is no big deal, and you choose to either minimize it or change the subject?

It's okay to acknowledge what you're good at. I'm not saying to be arrogant. I'm using this as an example of something that was told to me when I was *really* having a difficult time. This particular presentation was before 8,000 people. Speaking at this event were also people who were mentors and idols of mine, people whom I deeply respect. I had started comparing myself to them and thinking, "Well, I don't know if I have as much to offer as they do!"

Kim said to me, "When you start comparing yourself to somebody else, you immediately cut yourself in half, and when you do that, you block half of your ability to deliver your gift."

I didn't understand what he meant at first. He went on to say, "Think about it. When you compare yourself to somebody else, you have just cut yourself in half because one half of your brain is preoccupied with the other person, and the other half is occupied with you. You immediately cut in half what you're able to deliver."

Holy Moly! All of a sudden it made sense to me. What a huge insight!

Forget about them and just focus on you—that's tough enough! Most people don't need to worry about competition. You have enough competition between your right ear and left ear!!!

When it comes to your team (like in volleyball or tennis) you don't need anyone else on the other side of the net. You have enough problems on your own side of the net. I'm sure you know what I'm talking about.

You have enough going on with your own little voice. You don't have to worry about competitors that much. You don't need to worry about anybody but you.

You don't need to worry about your prospect or your boss, your spouse, your money issues, or any of that other stuff. All you have to do is work out what's going on inside of you.

If you handle that, the rest is easy! That's why authenticity is so important. The degree to which you can get closer to being yourself and stay true to it, is the degree to which you'll be able to deliver whatever it is you have inside to deliver.

Are you meant to teach people how to be Internet savvy? How to write? How to forgive? Is your gift being a great mom or dad? Whatever your gift is, be true to it and yourself, and realize that when you start worrying and comparing yourself to others, you cut yourself in half. If you compare yourself to five others, you cut yourself into fifths. So think about that for a second—who are you? Being you, I guarantee you, *is good enough.*

Robert Pante, one of my mentors, said it really well a long time ago. He said, "Look, you were put on this planet and given the best. You were not given plastic eyeballs and polyester skin. You were not given rubber bones. You were given the most incredible materials that make up your body. So inside a shell made of such incredible materials, wouldn't the contents be equally as good or even better?" Why would you create a five-million-dollar safe just to house a two-cent paper clip? That wouldn't make sense. Obviously, what's on the inside is even more valuable than what's on the outside."

What you've got on the inside is indeed good enough. That's why it's critical to battle the little voice that doubts it, that minimizes you and says you aren't good enough. In fact, there's probably so much good stuff in there that you're only utilizing about 10 percent of it. But if you could stay true to even that 10 percent, you'd be on your way. Be who you are. Be whoever it is you were meant to be. That's enough.

This brings up a myth that is a pet peeve of mine. I have seen it frustrate thousands of people over the years. You've heard the saying, "You can be whatever you want to be." Well, I'm here to tell you: That's a lie. That's a thought that can cause tremendous struggle in your life. You cannot be whoever you want to be!!

Take, for example, Shaquille O'Neal. Shaq is about 7'3" tall, and he weighs over 300 pounds. He's a center in the NBA. Now, let's just say that all of a sudden, Shaq decides that he wants to be a horse jockey. I think we all know there's no way this could happen. He's simply not designed for that. That's not his gift, so he *can't* be whatever he wants to be. (Not that I think he'd ever actually want to be that!)

> **You can't be whoever you want to be.**
> **You can be whoever you're "supposed to be."**

You can be whatever is inside of you, who you are intended to be. And for me it has become a lifelong journey to figure out what the heck that is.

You know, we spend a good portion of our lives being tested, analyzed, and diagnosed, whether it's a performance review at work, a personality profile test, a health physical, or one of the scores of other diagnostics designed to show you who you really are. Many times these interventions are designed to reveal your strengths and your weaknesses.

Yet, what are you usually told to do at the end of each test, particularly at work? To work on improving your weaknesses, right? Now, I'm here to tell you something. That is a colossal waste of time! It's hard enough to figure out what you're good at. Why would you spend your time trying to fix something that you're simply not genetically programmed to do?

One of my clients was a large bank in Canada. They called me awhile back and asked me to do some "etiquette training" for their investment bank analysts. I don't know if you know what an investment bank analyst is, but these are individuals who basically sit in front of a computer monitor and look at the market all day long. So my natural question to them was, why would they need etiquette training? They explained, "When we take them to client meetings, their shirt tails are hanging out, they're chewing gum, they don't listen. They're disheveled and even sometimes rude."

I was shocked, but not for the reason they were thinking. I said, "Why are you taking them to client meetings in the first place?"

"They're part of the team!" they exclaimed.

"Yeah, they're part of the team, but not designed to be in front of customers. They're analysts!" I said. "If you just put them in a cage with a computer and threw them meat once in a while, they would be happy. They're Chihuahuas!" (*SalesDogs* covers the five different types of Sales Dogs.) I went on to explain, "Chihuahuas are data freaks. They *don't like* talking to people. That's not their strength. It annoys them. And it not only upsets the client, it upsets the bank. Keep them away from clients, and let them do what they do best!"

The bank was adamant, "No, we want them to be trained in client etiquette."

I told them, "Well, you'd better find somebody else to do this because I guarantee you it's not going to make one bit of difference to their behavior. It's only going to annoy them."

I was right. It did. Why waste time trying to improve weaknesses when people are already loaded with strengths?

When I talk about weaknesses, I'm not referring to bad habits or a lack of skills. We all have those, and we all can improve upon them. I'm talking about natural strengths and weaknesses.

Results are a function of behavior. Behavior is a function of mindset and attitude. And all of that is a function of your conditioning and your talent. For example, everybody wants great results. So if becoming rich is a result that you want, how do you get it? How do you get great health or have great relationships?

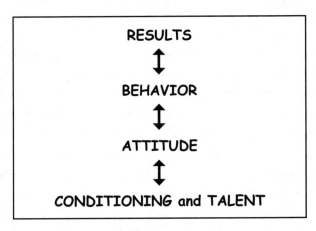

A lot of people say you have to have *desire*. And that's part of it, but it's not the whole truth. You can be full of desire to be someone that you're not, and we all know what you end up with—nothing but frustration. You can be full of desire to be rich and work your butt off to make it happen, but you still may be operating from bad conditioning or an ill-functioning little voice that says, for example ...

"Money doesn't grow on trees!"

"Money is the root of all evil!"

"If you want it done right, you've got to do it yourself."

"You can't trust anybody."

You can have all the desire in the world, but what you will end up with is frustration. It's like taking a four-by-four piece of wood and continually smacking yourself in the forehead. You're wondering why you're working so hard, trying to be a good person, doing the best you can, and still you don't get the result you want. It's because of inappropriate programming for what you want. You're operating from old conditioning, something that you were once told or that you once experienced in the past. Maybe it's something you learned five years ago that's no longer true today.

Everything in life changes quickly. So you have to change the programming of your little voice continually. You've got to manage it *all the time!* Because if you don't manage it, sooner or later, you're going to catch yourself operating based on old ideas.

You have to manage that little voice so that you're able to stay on course and discover what you are *supposed* to be—your genius. In *SalesDogs,* I talk about five different communication styles, or five different "breeds" of sales people: There's the chihuahua, the data freak I mentioned earlier; the poodle, who's the natural networker and schmoozer; the pit bull, who's the attack dog; the golden retriever, who loves to do favors for others and serve, hoping for reciprocity to ultimately swing in their favor; and finally, there's the basset hound, who has the ability to build instant one-on-one rapport.

No one breed sells or makes more money than the other. No one breed is a better communicator or a better marketer or a better business person or parent than the other. Each one has his own style. You've got to find yours, play to your strengths and feel good about them, without worrying about what others think.

The closer you come to being true to yourself, the more things around you will start to change. One thing you may ultimately realize in this process is that the people around you whom you thought were your friends and supporters may not be your friends anymore.

You may find that as you're seeking out better ways of being you, they're freaking out because you seem to be changing into a better person, which in turn challenges their standards and where they are in life. They may be quite comfortable where they are.

You know what probably most upsets them? The more authentic, confident, and congruent you become, the happier, freer, and lighter you are, and the higher your energy. Those people who have low energy and are miserable in their lives resent people who feel good about themselves. Some will do anything to try to bring you down. They'll say things like, "You shouldn't do that! That's not good for you. You've never done anything like that before, why are you doing it now? You'll fall flat on your face. I don't think this is good for you. How will that look to the group? What makes you so special? Are you too good for us now?"

As you attempt to break away from your past limitations, two things can happen: You either agree with your "friends" and give up on your quest for freedom and the changes you've undertaken, or you find new friends who are more supportive of you, the real you, as you continue on your path to success.

> **Bill Cosby once said, "I don't know the key to success,
> but I do know the key to failure is trying to please everybody."**

You can't please everybody. You have to please your spirit, the real authentic you. But saying that it's as simple as following steps one, two, and three would be absurd. That's a part of your lifelong journey. I'm still working on it myself, but I know that if I am diligent, I get closer all the time. Here's a suggestion that may help.

In Jim Collins' book *Good to Great,* he analyzed great companies. He studied their thirty-year histories: fifteen years prior to the significant "transition point" when they made the turn from a good company to a great company and fifteen years after that point.

Think about your own life. What have you been doing for the last five to fifteen years? What have you been training and preparing yourself to do? If today were *your* "transition point" and you made what Collins referred to as a "conscious decision to go from good to great," what would the next fifteen years look like? What will your "good to great" story be?

If you look at your own track record, you'll see that *you have been learning and growing.* You have had wins and magic moments, as well as setbacks. But through it all you are still standing, and somehow you're better today than you were before. Consciously or unconsciously, you have been preparing for greatness.

Many people can't see that big picture. Most people can only see what they're doing today. They're forced into survival mode. They force themselves into situations where they make money decisions based on what is directly in front them. They deal with the issues they've got right *now.* Like my partner Kelly Ritchie says, "Most people over-plan a day and under-plan a year." And if they under-plan a year, they *really* under-plan a lifetime.

But if you could sit down with a counselor, mentor, or a friend—someone who knows you well and will give you the ugly truth—what would that person tell you about *you?* If the two of you looked back fifteen, thirty years or more, and made a list of all the things you've done in your life, what patterns would emerge? Look at your experiences, your careers, your jobs, your ventures, and your hobbies. Where were the highlights in your life? What things did you do well? When were you "in the zone"? I'm not just talking about making money. When were you at your best?

If you can see the patterns emerge, you have just taken a step closer to finding the real you!

Have some other people, people you really trust, give you feedback. Ask each of them, "What do you think I'm really good at?" Make sure you tell them that you're not looking for BS here. Let them know you're very serious about this. And then, really listen to what they say, and be sure to pay attention to what your little voice says in response.

The little voice will typically say, "That's not really me!" because your little voice may have a hard time admitting that you're good at something.

This is another reason why it's tough to be yourself—because when people start getting close and giving you compliments like, "You did this so well. This is something you're really good at. You've changed my life!" you immediately think, "No, that was just circumstances. I was lucky. It really was no big deal. You're being too kind." You may want to minimize it.

> *Pay attention to the area of your life in which you receive the most compliments.*

For some reason, most of us are taught to believe that when we are given compliments or accolades, we should be humble; we're taught that you shouldn't brag about yourself. "Don't be vain." Now, I'm fine with being humble, but then people say "Listen and obey those who are in authority." ... "Remember that you're not better than anybody else ... people who are richer than you are smarter than you ... " you become conditioned to believe that you are somehow "less than."

So when you hear from someone else that you were great, you automatically think, "No, I'm not!" because you've been programmed the other way since you were a kid.

If you do nothing else today, do this: The next time someone gives you a compliment, ignore whatever your little voice is saying, and just say, "Thank you." Don't make excuses: the "buts," the "oh wells," or the justifications for why it's no big deal. Just say, "Thank you." And let your little voice deal with it until you learn to accept the win.

> *When someone pays you a compliment and your little voice starts chirping away with excuses, you are robbing yourself of a win and putting the brakes on acknowledging and leveraging your strengths.*

You don't have to stand on a soap box in the middle of the street, pound on your chest, and crow like a rooster. (Well, you can if you want to.) You just have to allow yourself to take the compliment and feel good about it.

Pay attention to the area of your life in which you receive the most compliments. I can honestly tell you that my family and I have a pretty awesome life. I'm blessed with great kids, my wife is an incredible life partner, and I have great partners and friends. Yet, I have to tell you that even after all these years, I'm still not clear what I'm supposed to be doing with my life, if you can believe that. I think I'm getting closer. I don't know that I'll ever really know, but it's all part of a life-long journey. It means management of my little voice will always be a part of my thinking.

I know I've said this before, but it's worth repeating. Bucky Fuller said:

> *"Your significance, (or your purpose in life) may remain forever obscured to you. But you can rest assured that you're fulfilling your purpose if you commit yourself to the highest advantage of others."*

You may never know what you're *really* supposed to do or what your real gift is. But if you're diligent enough about working on yourself and moving toward it, and all the while correcting, correcting, correcting as you find ways of getting into the arena where you do your best work, you'll get closer. And you'll likely find that you have more success surrounding you.

Along the way, you may shed some dead weight in the form of friends who have been holding you back. And remember, one of the biggest fears people have, the one that stops them from being authentic, is the fear that nobody will like what's really underneath. And honestly, that may sometimes be the case. When others see who you really are, in all your brilliance, honesty, and greatness, they may be intimidated. Some of them won't like you. They may resent you, they may be jealous of you, or they may just be upset that you've changed. The truth is, if that happens, they're really upset with themselves because you're feeling better than they are.

But most of the people around you will actually like you better, because true friends can see the greatness in you and they'll find it a relief to see it finally shine through. You'll also start attracting a group of friends who will really support who you're becoming. They'll give you accolades for being who you are. These are the people who will push you on to become more of who you can be.

You may go through several transitions in your lifetime. You already have. Just think about it. Do you still hang out with your friends from high school? You might, but it's pretty rare. And if you do, it's probably because those people still support who you are, not just who you used to be.

It pains me to see grown people still frustrated about what to do with their lives, still unhappy with what they're doing. They're still trying to play the corporate employee, when really what's inside is a raging entrepreneur, an idealist, an inventor, a writer, a fitness guru, or a poet. You have to be you because sooner or later you're going to run out of time, and then you'll be stuck listening for the rest of your life to the little voice chatter that says, "I should've, I would've, and I could've." And that's a nasty little voice. Once your time has run out, that's it. That's all you get.

So what if your little voice is *already* doing that? Tell it to shut up. Stop what you're doing, and then take a look at what you've been doing up until that point. Where have you had the biggest wins? And start leveraging that!!

For as long as I can remember, I've been fascinated with great leaders and in learning to be one. I found that leadership came naturally to me, even way back in Cub Scouts and then all the way through high school. I'm not sure why—I'm not tall, strong, or even that good looking. But I like to lead. I was president of my student class. I was student body president. I was captain of the track team and the cross-country team, and head field manager for the Ohio State football team.

And while speaking in front of groups still scares me a bit, for some reason, I enjoy it. I used to get queasy the week before any presentation. So why did I continue to put myself through it? I'm not quite sure. My wife still has to tell me,

"You're going to be fine. You're going to be great. Don't worry about it so much." To this day, even after twenty-seven years in this career, it still bugs me. But, for whatever reason, I keep looking back and finding this same affinity for being in front of lots of people—teaching and leading.

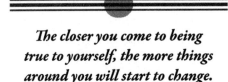

The closer you come to being true to yourself, the more things around you will start to change.

Despite my nervousness and doubt, I just knew that was where I was supposed to be. And it did NOT come easily!!! I worked hard to be the best I could be in those presentations, no matter how small or insignificant they were at the time. I had to rely on my own self-discipline and a tremendous amount of practice. I had to continually manage my little voice to get through it all.

I stood in the front of lots of rooms and talked to lots of people. At one point, I traced my experiences and looked at my track record; I found that those times when I was at my best were when I was in front of groups of people.

So then I thought, what if I spend more time doing that? I did. It then became apparent that I did my best work when I was actually teaching something, rather than just trying to sell something. I got the biggest kick out of teaching. I loved it. I spent four years learning to teach a great course that changed my life called "Money and You." It was created by a brilliant mentor of mine, Marshall Thurber. Robert Kiyosaki and I both studied and learned to teach it. We spent our own money to travel around the world teaching so we could become the best. That's how much we loved to teach business and personal development. The question always was, "What am I good at?" Today, I ask myself repeatedly, "What am I *best* at?" and "What do I have the most passion for?" Time and again, the same answer surfaces—teaching.

But after hundreds of thousands of people and thousands of businesses in more than twenty countries, the little voice in my brain said, "I'm tired. If I keep this up, I will wear out." There came a point when I literally flew around the world twice in opposite directions in less than ten days conducting training programs!!! I was in the U.S., Canada, Bangkok, Frankfurt, London, Japan, Singapore ... that's a lot of being in front of people.

It was time for another transition point. I realized there had to be a bigger game for me.

One little voice said, "I love to teach." Another little voice said, "But I'll wear out!" And yet a third little voice said, "Who says I have to do all the teaching?"

I also realized that of all the training that I do, some of the most profound results come from when *I'm teaching other people how to teach*. I really love taking average people and turning them into great presenters and trainers, and giving them the ability to be courageous and bold in a matter of seconds.

So then I thought, well, if I'm good at showing people how to teach, couldn't I show them how to teach the way that I teach? After all, if I'm great at this, couldn't my methods help them to be great, too?

That's why I launched SalesPartners, a worldwide system of franchise owners who teach entrepreneurs how to be rich. Our mission is to improve the quality of life for all humanity through a transformation of the marketplace.

So by reflecting, assessing, and linking my loves and my strengths together, I get closer every day to being the best me I can be, and to finally doing whatever it is that I'm supposed to be doing. All the while, I do my best to serve the greatest number of people possible at all times. It's an impossible task unless I remain diligent about managing my little voice, being authentic, and constantly refining by corrections.

I wish I could tell you that's all there is to it. I wish I could tell you that twenty years ago that this was my vision. There was no vision. There is no grand plan. I don't think the universe works that way. The universe consists of trial and error. It's about engaging and correcting, engaging and correcting. Put one foot in front of the other until you get where you need to go.

The bumble bee goes from one flower to another until it figures out that it likes roses better than daisies. Then it ditches the daisies and goes only for roses. My point here is that you may never figure it out completely, but if you stay true to who you are, to the best of your ability, eventually you'll get closer and your frustration will subside. The stress will lessen and the results will improve. The income, the energy, and the accolades will all increase. And if you can convince your little voice to accept those accolades and stay quiet long enough to say "Thank you" without minimizing it, your journey will accelerate.

> ### *You'll come closer to that real person inside you—*
> ### *the real gift, the real jewel inside.*

As I've repeatedly said, I have been blessed with great teachers and mentors. One of them, Robert Pante, is an expert in accessing that "inner jewel," particularly with young people.

It was incredible to watch Robert transform these kids. He pulled no punches with them; he was brutally honest with them about the effects of their actions and attitudes, but he was also just as honest when he spoke about their gifts, their "inner jewels"—the beauty inside each of them. He disregarded all the negative things that people had said about them for so many years, all the things that were supposed to be wrong with them, that they were disruptive and rebellious, and he made them into good things, things to be proud of. He showed them the greatness that was inside of them.

During some of the sessions, Robert and his team conducted "makeovers" with the kids, putting them in great clothes, giving them new hairstyles, making them look great so they could experience their own beauty and potential.

I remember Robert working with one kid who probably had thirty pierced rings in his face—in his ears, his nose, his eyelids, his tongue, his cheeks, and his lips. That hardware had been there for more than a year. He had never spoken to anybody about his problems, much less taken a ring out because someone asked him to. He mostly avoided people, shuffling around with his cap down over his eyes.

By lunchtime on the day he met with Robert, half the rings were out of his face. By the end of the day, his hair had been cut and all the rings were out. Nobody had even asked; he did it on his own. But most astounding was the change in his demeanor. This quiet, distant young man who hadn't spoken to anyone in the three days he had been with us was now engaging with others, sharing information with amazing articulation. He had always been good-looking, but now everyone knew it. He wore a huge smile on his face, making him almost unrecognizable to the group—except to Robert, who had seen it in him all along.

We occasionally do these types of makeovers in some of our programs. We bring in professionals, like hairdressers or makeup artists, to help bring out the physical beauty in people who can't see it in themselves. And what's so amazing isn't necessarily the physical transformation, although that's pretty extraordinary. But the most amazing part is the personality changes that come as a result. When you feel shining and beautiful on the outside, you feel more ready to share what's beautiful on the inside.

Have you ever noticed that you can easily see things in other people that they can't see in themselves? That means that others see things in *you* that you can't see in yourself as well. That is the theme of everything that we do. The goal is to bring out the genius in people and to help them realize their dreams. When people are truly letting themselves be the best they can be, it's exhilarating. There's no better feeling in the world. And when you're experiencing your true calling, using the gifts you were meant to use, you'll feel a rush like none you've ever felt.

Do it for yourself. Do it for your kids. Be a walking example of working to create an authentic, successful life. I see my life as having three parts. The first is my business, which provides my income and fulfills my mission on this planet. The second part, which is equally as important and is both my mission and my passion, is to have the happiest, healthiest family possible. The third one is to have the best health and fitness that I can have: mentally, emotionally, and physically. That means managing my body and managing my little voice. And I do this not only for myself, but for my kids.

Kids pick up on things a lot more quickly than they're given credit for. For example, one of our SalesPartners' franchise owners was working with a sandwich shop that employed several teenagers. The owner of this shop told us, "You can't teach fifteen-year-olds anything. They're not going to listen. It's not going to make any difference."

Within an hour or two of working with these fifteen-year-olds behind the counter, they had figured out how to make more money in tips, how to engage customers in conversation, and how to make their work fun. They went from making $2 per shift in the tip jar to $12–$15 per shift. And of course, at $15 per shift, do you think they were more engaged? Do you think that sales went up? How about the dollar amount per transaction? We had helped them to figure out how to have fun, make it a game, be themselves, and improve the business at the same time.

The key to success is being authentic ... being real.

Sometimes your spirit gets caged up inside. Maybe that's because sometime in the past, someone told you that it wasn't okay to just be yourself. The real you was too "out there," too unorthodox, too radical—too much. Slowly but surely, you locked your true self away so others would like you better and to protect yourself from getting hurt. But that was the past. Now's the time to let it soar. Be who you are supposed to be, regardless of what anyone else says or thinks.

To demonstrate this concept in some of our programs, we hold a wooden arrow right up to a person's neck and ask them walk into it. Now, the arrow won't hurt them, but the little voice in each of their brains says it's going to kill them. *They walk into it.* We teach them how to be resourceful and anchor success. And when they ultimately break the arrow, suddenly all of the things that their little voice told them that they couldn't do, that they weren't good enough to do or be, all those things disappear in the snap of an arrow. All that crap just disappears.

For some people, it's very emotional. They might even cry. Many just go into shock, and later, when that shock wears off, the tears appear. And that's a sign that they're free. Because many people's spirits have been caged up for a long time, and the spirit was always meant to be free.

The reason some people become cynical is because, at some level they know their spirit is caged up and that time's running out. The chance to truly experience their own greatness seems to become more and more distant. Don't let that happen to you. In the words of Dr. Martin Luther King, Jr. in his famous "I Have a Dream" speech, "When we let freedom ring, from every village, from every hamlet, from every state and every city, we will be able to speed up that day when all of God's children ... will be able to hold hands and sing in the words of the old Negro spiritual, 'Free at last, free at last, thank God almighty we are free at last.'"

I wish all of you reading this book to be free at last. And the way to do this is simply to be you.

***The biggest reason to learn little voice mastery
is to get back to being who you really are.***

You are supposed to have a great life—to have great friends, a lot of money, and incredible relationships. Struggle comes when you deviate from that path.

What I do know is that the shortcut along that path is getting rid of the little voice that stops you by doing the following:

- Worrying about what other people think about you;

- Not letting you acknowledge your wins;

- Not enabling you to say "thank you" upon receiving a compliment;

- Not letting you see those things that you do really well.

Change those little voices, and you are on the road to freedom.

Need 2 understand this.

"If u cheat on U" (by breaking your Rules
... There's a mess, a muddle about
all this setting rules .. 4 myself.
etc. because I change my
mind ... and I am _flexible_ ....
I Ask my Silent Inner Partner 2
provide an answer. ...

Set a code of honour that will hold
under emotional pressure. (remember
high emotions, low intelligence.)
like i Never leave a job half-done
Complete tasks.

  Sticks 2 your rules → Rudder ⊛

Leaders have a Working set of Rules
that work 4 them - in other words
 a Code of Honour that Keeps them
accountable, reliable.

Use NLP on this Chapter 7. use all
the Resources: Time line. Swissth ...
etc . .... Use hypnosis HERICKsonian
              approach.
    . Re-framing ...

I DO WHAT I SAY I AM GOING 2 DO

I START MY CODE OF HONOUR

My Rules:

How do I keep track of Time

Money

Food

Water I Drink

Coffee

Tea

health - career - Relax - wealth

no booze - no smoking.
yoga . drinking - daily .
. study NLP + hypnosis,
daily .

The higher the Performance, the tighter the rules have 2 B (see germany)

Accountability:
Keeping Your Promises to Yourself

Beeing accountable 2 yourself is the most powerful thing 4 yourself

The fastest way to manage your little voice is to make yourself accountable. In other words, to do what you say you are going to do. There have to be certain standards that you're not willing to compromise, that you're willing to be answerable to. A set of goals, numbers, measuring points, if you will, that you are willing to strive for. It could be revenue, weight, numbers of sales calls ... anything. And in order to make that work, you have to have a set of personal rules so that when your little voice starts going south on you, you have something that keeps you from straying too far from your goals. It's called a Code of Honor.

These rules need to hold you in place even when your emotions are high and your intelligence is low, so that you're protected from the negative little voice that freaks out in the face of emotional crises.

Recently, I met with a very successful man who owns quite a few successful franchises. He goes into stores that are failing, buys them, and turns them around. I asked him what he'd ad observed in the stores he'd purchased.

"Well," he said, "in stores that are failing, you typically have absentee owners, or owners who have abdicated their responsibility to others and are not personally accountable."

I've spent some time observing how this gentleman operates, and I can tell you that every single day, he checks the numbers on all twenty of his stores. He puts them in rank order, he posts them in his office, and the next morning, he sends those results out to all the stores so they each know exactly how they stand in relation to the rest of the group. Everyone knows what their numbers are. All the managers see how close they are to breaking even, how much profit they're actually making, and whether or not they're on target for that year in terms of producing the amount of revenue they want. That's called accountability.

The first important thing to point out is that successful accountability is based on frequency—he does this *every day*. Secondly, they're held accountable to a set of goals. They see where they stand every single day.

The problem is, most people are not accountable, or if they are, the standards they're accountable to are fairly low. And there are lots of reasons why that is. The truth is that many times your little voice doesn't want to be held accountable because that forces you to look in the mirror and see the ugly truth that perhaps you're not ready to face. Maybe the problem is your weight. Maybe it's your finances. Maybe it's your business. Maybe it's your health. Whether it's a bathroom scale, a financial statement, or the truth from a respected source, real feedback can be painful.

Yet, without hard facts and a high level of accountability to goals, standards, and numbers, it's virtually impossible to improve upon anything. However, there are those people who avoid accountability, and instead navigate their businesses, their health, and their lives based on "how it feels." I don't know about you, but if I did that, my path would look like a roller coaster. Gut feelings have their place, certainly, but they're momentary. Numbers don't lie.

Accountability keeps your little voice in check
and forces it to work in your favor. It forces you to see the truth.

Accountability boils down to two categories. The first category is your numbers, or your **stats.** These could be your financial numbers, your sales, your income, your expenses, your caloric intake, your resting heart rate, your blood pressure, your weight ... anything that you can measure.

The second form of accountability is your **behavior.** With every organization and individual that I have worked with over the years, the single most powerful way to ensure behavioral accountability is through what we call a Code of Honor. In the book *The ABC's of Building a Business Team That Wins,* we show you how to create a Code of Honor in your business and your personal life. You learn how to take ordinary people and turn them into a championship team by setting up a set of rules that force people to be the best they can be.

How does this apply to you and your little voice? Well, first of all, you should have a personal Code of Honor—a personal set of rules that you are unwilling to compromise in the areas of your life that are important to you, like your health, your wealth, your business, and your relationships.

A rule typically found in a team's Code of Honor would be, "Never abandon a teammate in need." If you were to create a rule for your personal Code of Honor that exemplifies this idea, it might read, "Never give up on yourself," or "Never quit until you've achieved your goal." Another Code of Honor rule that enforces accountability would be, "Be responsible—no blaming or finger-pointing." That works

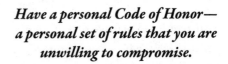

Have a personal Code of Honor— a personal set of rules that you are unwilling to compromise.

for team codes and personal codes. Others might be, "Be on time," or "Be willing to have others call you on your breaches of the code."

This last rule is important because to achieve success, partnership is a must. I have never met anyone who succeeded in any endeavor without trusted partners, colleagues, mentors, teammates, or companions. In other words, share your Code of Honor with the significant other people in your life so that if you break the rules, there's someone there to call you on it.

Always agree to tell the whole truth, 100 percent of the time. Operate out of 100 percent integrity. Never break a promise. Study and practice whatever you're looking to master for at least two hours per week. Whatever rules you create for yourself, stick to them.

I have had a lot of clients say to me initially, "I/we have rules already. We need something more." I quickly respond by reminding them that Arthur Anderson and Enron had rules, too. The problem was that even though they had rules, when executives and managers started to break those rules, nobody called them on it. Nobody said, "You're out of line. You have to correct that." And as a result, both institutions went under in a publicly humiliating way. And I can cite many other examples in business.

The bottom line is that you have to be willing to call yourself on it when you break a rule you've created, and you need to have others call you on it as well if you are going to really be accountable.

If you've got a Code of Honor, a set of rules for yourself that says you won't smoke or drink or cheat on your diet, and then someone sees you breaking your own rules, why would they want you on their team? If *you* cheat on *you,* the most important person of all, what would you do to your teammates? Is that how you'd act under pressure?

So in order to manage the little voice, you've got to have a level of accountability that keeps the little voice from lying, denying, or altering the facts. The easiest way to do that is to set up a set of rules, behavioral rules, in a Code of Honor. Every great team and great individual has a set of rules, a Code of Honor, so that under emotional pressure, that holds them in place.

Other rules in a personal Code of Honor might say, "Never abandon a task in the middle," "Never seek sympathy or acknowledgment," "Don't leave a job half-done," or "Don't look for pity when you need to get on with the job." Those rules will get you through difficult times. Stick to your rules, and they'll be your rudder, guiding you when life gets stormy and the waters get murky. Most great leaders and companies thrive because they have a working set of rules that keeps everyone accountable.

Time

What are your numbers? What do you keep track of? How about time? How much time is really productive? How much time is spent doing useless things? What is your resting heart rate? What is your blood pressure, and what are you doing to improve it? How far are you walking or running every day? What are you eating? What's your caloric intake? Do you see what I mean? *Food*

Money

Do you do your own financials? How often? If it's not you, who does them? Is it once a quarter when it's too late, or once a year when it's way too late? Or is it like our successful business owner-friend who does them every day?

I always tell people that the most powerful sales motivational tool of all for me used to be the Monday morning sales meeting. I learned that years ago when I worked at the Burroughs Corporation.

Every Monday morning, you had to put your prospects up on the board, show all the deals you were going to close, and forecast how much you were going to sell that week. Heaven help the guy who had the same prospect up more than three weeks in a row without closing. He'd get booed out of the room. On Thursdays and Fridays, people were running all over town getting new prospects, not because they wanted to make money so much as they just didn't want to be humiliated in front of everybody else on Monday morning.

Being accountable to yourself is very powerful. But if you want to take it to the next level, surround yourself with a team that you have to be accountable to and that will hold you to your commitments. In business, a team is critical to have financial success. To have optimal health, you should have a personal trainer, nutritionist, physician, and others who can support you on your journey. The people in your relationships are part of your team. And in all those teams, what are your rules and who holds you accountable to them?

For our two young boys, we have a set of rules posted on the refrigerator, for which they are accountable. There are rules like, "You may not destroy other people's property," "You must respect your coach, your teachers, and parents," and "You can't beat up on your little brother." If they break those rules, they get called on it. And on the other side of the sheet, there's a set of consequences. The first time it happens, they lose electronics for a week. The second time it happens, they lose yo-yo classes. The third time, they lose football, and so on. We go on with this until the message gets across. We're not into spanking or corporal punishment. That sends a different kind of message. But we want to teach them to be accountable and responsible for who they are and what they do.

In life, if you're not accountable, there are consequences whether you like it or not)!

In every country there's a set of rules about what is permissible and what is not. The problem is that, here in the United States especially, it's easy to NOT be accountable. In fact, it seems you couldn't starve to death if you wanted to. If you're out of work, someone will stuff food in your mouth, put you on welfare, or put you in a shelter. You'll be taken care of, somehow, by the government or someone else. So part of our conditioning is that there's no need to be accountable.

> **Always agree to tell the whole truth, 100 percent of the time especially to yourself.**

The truth is that if you're going to have success in your life—financially, emotionally and physically—the higher your level of accountability, the higher your performance will be and the better your results.

The first car I drove was a 1963 Chevy 2 Nova convertible, whose maximum speed was about 50 miles per hour downhill. It was a great car, but it wasn't what I'd call "high performance." And it didn't take much to fix it. Crescent wrenches and screwdrivers did the job.

On the flipside, my wife worked at Northrop in the F-18 fighter plane division. The rivets are actually packed in dry ice before they're put in the fuselage of the aircraft because the tolerance level needs to be that tight. They want to make sure that when the plane is flying at Mach 3 at high altitude, the rivets don't fall out of the aircraft. That would be a problem.

So compare the '63 Chevy to the F-18. Which has the higher performance?

The higher the performance, the tighter the rules have to be. And the bigger your organization or team, the tighter those rules have to be. My friend Robert Kiyosaki says it well: "The size of your organization is directly related to your ability to enforce the rules."

Now, when I say you have to be accountable, I don't mean that you have to be perfect all the time, because that's not possible. I don't mean that your numbers always have to look good, because your numbers won't always look good. Accountability simply means that you're willing to face the music. You're willing to admit to your mistakes just as often as you'll admit to your successes. Most people either never look at their numbers or only look when things are good.

For every up, there is a down. For every in, there is an out. By the same token, you have good and bad numbers. You have good days and bad days. You must have a willingness to see the whole thing.

My partner Kelly Ritchie says that in any business, it takes three months of seeing what's working and what's not for any patterns to emerge. The reason for accountability is that over time, if you log your numbers and keep close track of what you're doing, you'll see a definite pattern of your habits and the results they generate.

For example, let's say you're keeping track of your finances. Every week, you review your income as well as your expenses. You see these week in and week out. Over three months, you may see that your income typically spikes between the first and second week, and your expenses spike in the last week of the month. And you notice that the overall result is that you're always out of money. Why is that? Maybe you notice that when it comes to expenses, the minute you get any money you start indulging like crazy, so that when all the bills come at the end of the month, you don't have enough money to pay them. But without reviewing the results frequently over time, you won't see the recurring patterns of habit emerge. At that point, correction and improvement become a guessing game.

It's the same thing with your health. You may find that at a certain time of the day you're better at working out. You also notice that during another part of the

In TRACK IT — — — and I am on TRACK on Target of my Goal

day or certain types of days, or in certain types of weather, you may eat more. If you don't track it, it becomes tough to reach your fitness goals because you typically cannot see the patterns when you're in them.

You must have statistics to drive your results. Why? Because if you were to graph your emotional feelings about your weight, your health, your family, your finances, or your business, each of those graphs would probably look like a roller coaster. And basing your decisions on the peaks and the valleys of that roller coaster would be ridiculous in any kind of business. If you have an accountability system where you're watching your stats, then it's easier to stay on target for achieving your goals. For salespeople, the stats could include things like how many calls you're making, how many appointments you schedule, and how many presentations you're making. *How many galleries I send my images + CV.*

A friend of mine from Texas has a great expression. He says "Everybody wants to go to heaven, but nobody wants to die." Everyone wants to be successful and enjoy the fruits of success, but nobody wants to go through the difficult times or look at their ugly blemishes along the way.

Most people don't want to look in a mirror. Many don't want to see their poor results that intimately because they already have a sense that they aren't that good and it would only depress them. Plus, they definitely don't want anyone else to see them. Yet without those stats, hope fades to fatigue, which fades to frustration, which ends up in defeat.

Therefore, you have to have something that's stronger than the little voice. It's like having a police force out there to be stronger than the criminals. The police enforce a set of rules created by the community to maintain order. So even if you see a red light and you want to run through it, you're not going to because there's something out there that's stronger than your little voice, and that something will give you a ticket—or worse. They're called consequences. It's about being accountable to a third party, in this case a Code of Honor or a set of rules.

ADULT SELF.

The Ten Commandments are a set of rules that say things like, "Thou shalt not kill," "Thou shalt not commit adultery," or "Thou shalt not steal." These rules are all deeply embedded in Judeo-Christian society. Islam also has a code, and so do

They are all expressed in the negative and the unconscious does not process negatives

Buddhism, Confucianism, and all other faiths. These codes have been around for a long time and are designed to last. Accountability creates that longevity, and it helps to bring people from different walks of life into a common understanding and culture. Those groups or organized movements that don't have strict rules of conduct and behavior don't last or proliferate for long.

So here's a task:

Set up a personal code, a set of rules that you're willing to write down and put on paper in a prominent place. Share them with other significant people in your life, people to whom you're willing to be accountable and have call you on breaches of that code. It will create a sort of third-party "police force" that will help you to manage your little voice.

On our team, we are committed to holding each other accountable. Personally, I have several friends who do the same for me. And if I'm not being real, they'll call me on it!

For example, I have been known to keep my opinions to myself because I don't want to hurt people's feelings. Yet if I do that, people may not get the feedback they need from me. When that happens, my teammates and friends get all over me: "What are you doing? I'm calling you on that right now. I don't care if it's not comfortable, you gotta do it!"

And you know what? It works. A great teacher told me years ago, "If you want to be a master, you have to surround yourself with people who ask more of you than you ask of yourself." That's accountability.

In America, we have documents that keep the nation accountable. They're called the Constitution and the Declaration of Independence. We have many codes of law that are designed to keep us accountable to each other and to the government. Yet citizens have often observed that the very people charged with enforcing and defending those rules are also the ones who tend to perpetrate the biggest breaches of the code, and then refuse to be accountable for it and lie. That is perhaps why voter turnout in the U.S. is so low.

So ?: Though shalt (Not) kill ..etc - - -
No wonder we are where we are

If you break your own code, people lose faith in you. And you will ultimately lose faith in yourself if you develop a track record full of broken agreements with yourself. You, too, will stop showing up to "vote" for yourself. Each broken agreement strengthens the little voice that says, "I told you so," "It's no big deal, you'll get around to it later," or "It wasn't all that important, anyway."

I don't know about you, but I have my own Code of Honor, or set of rules, that acts as an independent "police officer" inside of me. It's stronger than I am. So when my emotions go up and my intelligence goes down, it keeps me doing what I know I should do.

The Code of Honor protects me from me.

I can't emphasize that enough. In a sane moment, when all your positive little voices are lined up in agreement, you can easily develop a set of standards for behavior, a set of numbers or a reporting system. But when your little voices are in that state of mind, you probably don't need a code to hold you in check in that moment. It's when you're under pressure, when life is hitting you in the face and it feels like you're getting squeezed that you'll need that code.

It's like the Marine Corps. They drill their code over and over because when bullets are flying by your ears, your emotions are red-lining and your desire to run for your life might run out of control. But because their code is firm about never abandoning teammates in need, Marines stick together under extreme pressure because they've drilled it so many times. You can do the same thing for yourself.

Now, this sounds like a pretty heavy chapter. It sounds like I'm suggesting that you post lists all over the bathroom mirror, on the refrigerator, throughout your day planner and just about everywhere else. But really, I'm not. It's actually pretty simple. You only need a few good, powerful personal rules.

Take my finances, for example. I get a financial statement every single week, and I'm accountable to those numbers. My SalesPartners team is accountable for their numbers every single week, too. They do the same thing for their clients, and their clients do the same thing for their own salespeople. That's because what's on the inside must be congruent to what's on the outside.

Again, the rules can be very simple. Many of them you already have, but don't take seriously enough sometimes. Some of the rules that you have within your relationships, your family, your business, or with yourself (for instance, with regards to your health) may serve the same purpose.

One rule everyone should have is, "Celebrate all wins."

Another is, "Keep your stats."

Or maybe, "Never abandon yourself, or teammates, when in need."

These are all simple but common rules that can apply to anybody. And of course, for some specific areas in your life, you'll have special rules. But the important thing is that you have rules and you track your numbers, because numbers don't lie. Talk is cheap, and you can end up convincing yourself of anything, really, until you look at the numbers.

Being accountable really boils down to three things:

1. Willingness to admit to your mistakes, being willing to look in the mirror and admit to both mistakes and wins. Be willing to own it. You've got to be able to admit when you've screwed up. This is not about beating yourself up; it's about owning your actions, good and bad.

2. Being thankful for what you have. Be thankful that you're living and breathing and for your ability to actually admit your mistakes, and your ability to do something about them.

3. Committing to good deeds or acts that you will perform today, tomorrow, and for the rest of your life.

So admit to your mistakes and own them. Be thankful for what you've got—all the good things that surround you, and the resources and opportunities to correct mistakes. And finally, commit to doing something good with your gifts.

What good things will you do for yourself? For your family? For your business? For your community? For the planet?

As an organization, we volunteer our time to go into schools and teach kids the lessons and skills of entrepreneurship, financial literacy, and giving back to the community. We donate time, money, products, and services for the purpose of improving the quality of life for everyone through transformation of the marketplace. Most of all, we have the gift of teaching. And we spend every moment committed to teaching people how to transform their lives, find their real selves, and become the huge being they were meant to be.

What are the good things you will do? Maybe you'll spend some time with an older person who's feeling lonely or abandoned and engage him or her in conversation. That's an act of kindness. Yet your little voice may try to divert you with a thousand reasons why you can't or won't go out of your way for that person, like "I'm too busy," or "Somebody else can do it; it's not my job." That's when you need to rely on those standards you've set for yourself.

We do this every Friday night with our kids when we sit down at dinner. We ask them, "What good deeds did you do this week?" Ben might say, for example, that he helped the teacher clean up the classroom. Zach might say that he fed the dog. Whatever. It doesn't matter how big or small it is. The point is that they get into the habit of being accountable.

You need to be accountable for what you've done and for what you're going to do. So accountability is for the past, present, and future.

What have you done? Be willing to admit to it. If it wasn't what you said you'd do, what are you going to do to correct that? Keep track, because actions speak louder than words.

The whole idea is to take action. Talk is cheap. And so as I wind down this section on accountability, here's a story to illustrate what I mean.

There's a high school football team near Salt Lake City, Utah. Some of the leaders from that community bought fifty copies of my book, *The ABC's of Building a Business Team That Wins* and gave them to each of the kids on the team. The kids were told to read it and study it together during the summer weight-training sessions before the season started. They studied it, discussed it, and created a Code of

Honor for their team. I didn't know about this team until I happened to be in Salt Lake for another program. Upon my arrival, I was intercepted by one of the team member's parents and asked if I could do a little talk for the team. Upon hearing their story, I was honored to accept.

It was after practice as I stood before this group of young men, seniors in high school, and they showed me the Code of Honor they had written. The coaches hadn't helped them do it—the team had done this together. They had created rules like, "Never abandon a teammate in need," "Always cover each others' backs," and "Be willing to call each other on breaches of the code."

I asked one of the senior linebackers on the team what he thought was the biggest lesson they learned from the book and the creation of the code. He said, "We learned that the most important rule was being able to call yourself in front of the team."

He was right. Being able to publicly admit when you screw up, when you've blown it in front of others who might be affected by it, is very difficult, but so important.

I have to say that it brought tears to my eyes because, of all the speaking engagements I've done around the world in dozens of countries, I was never so moved as I was by these teenagers who sat there bright-eyed, some with tears in their own eyes, talking about the first game they went into with their code. They explained that they had gone into the game as complete underdogs against the defending state champions. Yet, in overtime, they went on to beat them.

I asked them, "How did it feel to do that?"

"We knew we were going to win because we had a code," they said. "Because we knew our mates on either side wouldn't let us down."

Here's a group of teenagers who decided to hold themselves accountable. They created a code for themselves. They call each other on it publicly. Their passion and their heart filled my soul.

Even though I have stood in front of thousands of people, worked directly with some of the most powerful business leaders in the world, I have never been as honored and moved as I was in that sweaty locker room. In an age of complexity and change, challenge and distractions, temptations and shortcuts, these young men had taken a stand for each other. They knew the meaning of team, code, and loyalty. It was the backbone of something worth defending. It was something that will make them different from most of their friends. It was something that they will carry with them all of their lives into every relationship.

What are you doing? I'll wager that most of you reading this book are older than they were. Some of you might be double or triple their age. So I ask you, are you as accountable as those young men?

And if the little voice in your brain says, "Oh that's different. They're kids. That's just football," then maybe you need to stand in that locker room for a while and have those young men talk to you. Because they said something I will never forget, that "... when all the smoke clears, the only thing you really have left is your honor."

> *In order to manage the little voice, you've got to have a level of accountability that keeps the little voice from lying, denying, or altering the facts.*

Be accountable to your team, your family, your business, and your community. The more people you're accountable to, the more people you'll be serving, the greater the impact you'll have, and the more reciprocity you'll experience. You'll have a significant ripple effect on others around you, you'll make more of a difference, and your life will become richer. If you can't be accountable to anybody else, at least be accountable to your kids. And most importantly, be accountable to yourself.

Don't let yourself down. You've probably done that too many times in your life already. Set up a code that holds you accountable to you, and hold yourself to it through thick and thin. You may blow it ... that's okay. Simply admit it, correct it, and get on with it. If you blow the same commitment more than a couple times, seek outside support. That could be a part of your Code of Honor. And when you do that, you'll see your level of play increase, and your speed and effectiveness will increase, too.

A few of the friends that you had may no longer be your friends because they'll want to pull you back down. They'll want you to be the same sloppy self that you were before. Don't let that happen. As I said before, you deserve to be around the best.

With your set of rules, create numbers that you can be accountable to, that force you to be the best that you can be. With daily and weekly frequency (the more frequent, the better), those numbers and rules will be like looking in the mirror day in and day out. They'll tell you how you're *really* doing. Just by having read this, you've demonstrated that you're willing to take the next step. So sit down and do the things that I just asked you to do, and you will already have raised the standards for yourself.

I know you can do this because that's why you picked up this book. Part of you has been waiting for this for a long time, just waiting for you to step up to the plate. It takes a tremendous amount of courage to look in the mirror sometimes, but you've got to do it. And you've known that all along. So, let's get on with it, okay?

From: Flabby, Slobby, Sloppy
to: trim, elastic, tight, timed timing
fit. in mind/body
at home, in finance, in Art
in the world. —
Strike the Balance
Set a balanced Code of Honour

How to Remove the Cap that Your Little Voice Puts on Your Results

Fifty-five thousand dollars of real sales and income in 10 minutes!! Over half a million dollars in sales in 4 days with no product knowledge, no business cards, no website and in a team of total strangers speaking different languages and dealing in multiple currencies. How is this possible? How is it possible that in some of our programs (such as the one referred to here) that average individuals can generate more income in 4 days or 10 minutes than most of them can in 4 months or a year?

It's because what I know and have experienced in over 20+ years of business and training is that inside you is a gigantic being capable of way more than you can imagine or that you give yourself credit for. I do not know you personally, but I suspect that you have no idea how big you really are.

That is why for most of my life, I have done my best to discover how to reclaim that bigness of spirit and capability and to teach others how to claim it. Certainly the purpose of this book is to give you the tools for removing the limiting little voices that sabotage and confine your brilliance.

Let me give you an example of what I am talking about. Have you ever been in a large auditorium where there were hundreds or even thousands of people and in the midst of the hubbub you hear a baby cry? You could hear it, right? Let me ask you, did the baby have a microphone?? Of course not. You could hear that infant cry amidst all the chaos. Why? Because you come into this world as a huge being. Your presence and intention is huge. At the same time you heard that baby cry, you probably could not hear the person talking a few seats away from you.

So how do you reclaim that bigness? Why is it that even with hard work, diligence, personal and responsibility that the results that you are looking for are so far away? As I have said before, if you can just get the little voice out of the way, the big you will emerge. In chapter six, we talked about how RESULTS are a function of Behaviors, Attitude and Conditioning.

Since the initial writing of this book, the realization of an additional element has proven to make incredible differences in the ability to achieve unprecedented levels of wealth, health, joy and size of game for thousands. I want to share it with you. Are you interested? I'll bet you are.

This insight and process I am about to share is again ... not original. As I have said many times, I think that any success that I have had in my life is because of being blessed by incredible mentors, teachers, and coaches who have been relentless, disciplined, and nearly unreasonable in their coaching and mentoring of me.

Recently one of those individuals is my fitness trainer Mack Newton (www.macknewton.com). Having both Super Bowl and World Series rings and having trained some of the world's foremost world-class athletes, I have been honored to be coached by him as well.

His take on this unleashing of peak performance is summed up simply. He says that your BELIEFS (formed by conditioning) are the result of your

SELF-CONCEPT—or how you see yourself. I will do my best to explain this and, as I do, I suspect your little voice will start chirping in. You may even experience some emotional response. That is GOOD!! If that happens, it means that you are gaining mastery and unlocking even more of who you are supposed to be. Trust me!

He says it simply: "YOU CAN NEVER OUTPERFORM YOUR SELF-CONCEPT." In other words, no matter what results you are striving for in your life—money, health, relationships, success—no matter how hard you try, you can never exceed your vision of yourself. If you hold that you are not a good salesperson or that you cannot really sell, or that you are just too dumb to learn it, or it's "just not you!!!" you will NEVER generate the income that you desire in business.

If you hold that you are too old, too young, not smart enough, too fat, too skinny, too dysfunctional or whatever, your results will always have a lid on them. When he told me that, it all began to make sense; all those times of success, all those folks who won, and all those great people who strove hard with great intentions, but never seemed to get their just deserves. Know what I mean?

Mack explained further. He said that your SELF-CONCEPT is made up of three things.

1. Your SELF-IDEALS. These are the characteristics that you want to have that you typically observe in others that you consider to be role models in certain areas. For me, I strive for the leadership qualities of Martin Luther King or John F. Kennedy. I strive for the business and money prowess of several mentors in my life. I long for the wit, peace and at-one-ness of the Dalai Lama, the patriarchal guidance of my father and grandfather, the health and fitness of Mack Newton, the little voice mastery of Alan Walter, etc. It doesn't mean I have mastered those characteristics, but it is what I strive for or hold as ideals. It also does not mean that I idealize the negative characteristics of those individuals—just what I want for me.

TO DO: Identify who your role models are ? If you were to make a portfolio of the characteristics, skills, and attitudes that would make the ideal YOU, who are those individuals that exhibit them? They may not be people you know personally, perhaps who you have read about or studied. Make a list !!!!

2. The second part of your SELF-CONCEPT according to Mack is your SELF-IMAGE. It is what you see in yourself when you look in the mirror. Do you hold yourself as a great parent, friend, lover, partner? Now I know the little voice throws us doubts from time to time about all of that, but at the end of the day after you have told your little voice to STOP when it is beating you up. Do you see a beautiful body staring back at you hungry to adapt the eating and exercise habits that will reveal the real you? Do you really hold that you are a brilliant business person simply learning the ropes? Do you see yourself as a great communicator with a never ending thirst to learn? Or do you simply see a person with bad habits, too old and too slow to change—not smart enough, not lucky enough or whatever? See what I mean about the "little voice"? It may be hurting you in ways you don't even know!!!!

TO DO: Create a list of affirmations that override that negative self talk. Things like "I like myself, I can do this!" "I am an awesome salesperson getting better every time I practice. I am a strong person who can take on anything the world dishes out to me. I love people and am a great relationship builder." You get the picture. When stuff comes up, repeat the affirmations again and again, and you will suddenly find things getting easier and flowing toward you.

3. Thirdly, your self-concept is comprised of your SELF-ESTEEM. How you feel about yourself. How much you like yourself at the very core of your personality. Do you really love yourself or do you continue to beat the daylights out of yourself? Do you treat yourself well and with honor or do you abuse and discount yourself? Do you really like who you are?

For example, if you are trying to lose weight, you KNOW that an extra piece of chocolate cake is not good for you—right? But your little voice says, "One more bite couldn't possibly make a difference." The only reason you would take that bite is if your self-esteem is low. Why else would you KNOWINGLY hurt yourself? Your willingness to do things that you know you should not do is a sure sign of low self-esteem and self-concept. So it isn't so much about the cake. That decision just trashed your self-esteem, your self-concept, and took a serious bite out of your ability to produce other results in your life.

See what I mean about the "little voice"? It is sneaky and sinister sometimes. There are a myriad of ways it is killing you and you don't even see it!!

So in order to produce the results you want, to accomplish the dreams in your life that you so much deserve and to even help others achieve their dreams, you have got to preserve your self-esteem at all costs. Do not let your little voice demean you. Do not let it discount your best efforts.

TO DO: I am not saying to be easy on yourself!! Be tough on yourself. Demand the best. Never quit. Push harder. But do NOT beat yourself up, do not insult yourself, do not let the little voice take down your brilliant image of you and do not let it treat you like a second-class citizen.

And for sure when working with others, challenge them hard, but do not demean them. I watched Mack working with one of his young Taekwondo students (age 8). This young fellow did not have a good attitude this particular day. His workout was slow, he was tired and clearly was having difficulty paying attention. Mack got right in his face and said something I will never forget and, that as a parent, I will strive to remember. He said, "I love you to death and you are an incredible kid. You and I both know that. But that behavior that you are exhibiting is not going to be tolerated and has got to go!" I saw a combination of tears, respect, and resolve in his little eyes as he went to the floor to do his obligatory sets of knuckle push-ups. I remembered his words: "Preserve self esteem at all costs." He separated the negative behavior from the person, thus preserving that young boy's self esteem. Wow! And the kids LOVE him!

Why am I so big on this? In a recent program of independent business owners working with a large and very reputable network marketing company, it just blurted out of me as never before. I was asked why I continue to teach. Why do I continue to create programs that get people to accomplish so much in such a small period of time?

I do it because after 27 years and hundreds of thousands of people like you. I KNOW HOW BIG YOU ARE AND HOW HUGE YOUR SPIRIT IS. You don't see it but I do! That is why I will do whatever it takes to put you in scenarios that force you to be successful so that your self- concept is altered once and for all. So that no matter what your little voice thinks, if I can move it out of the way long enough and force you to make money, see your brilliance, feel your bigness. It may scare you, but it will alter your self image forever. You can never deny what you have accomplished.

That is your job as a teacher, parent, leader, friend.

There is a giant spirit and being inside of you. Through affirmations, repetition, little voice mastery techniques and certainly by putting yourself in challenging situations, it will emerge. Take the time to review your self-ideals, your self-concept and establish a Code of Honor that protects you from you. That forces you to challenge yourself but to treat yourself with honor and respect. If you do, your self concept will rise and as it does, so will your results.

Solutions for the Four Reasons People Fail

People really fail for the same set of reasons. And once you know the little voice processes for handling them, your world will begin to stream floods of resources, relationships, wealth, health and joy to you. The good news is that there are really only four main reasons. Some of these reasons we have covered, but there are a couple of reasons why people fail that you may not suspect.

#1 is FEAR.

By now, that should seem obvious as we have talked about this a lot. It's the little voice's fear about what others think, fear of looking stupid, fear of being ostracized or fear of losing. The second one is not is not so obvious. It was pointed out to me by Alan Walter extremely well. It was pointed out to me by Alan Walter extremely well.

#2 is FATIGUE.

You just run out of juice. You get to a place in your life where you can actually SEE your dream in the distance. You have the life experience. You have the level of maturity, but you're tired and out of energy or you cannot sustain it for any extended period of time. Yet to accomplish your dreams, mission or whatever you really want takes lots of energy.

As a result, you end up cynical, frustrated, talking about what 'could have been' rather than what can be. It's like a marathon runner slogging through all those long miles able to see the finish line waaay off in the distance, but not seeming to get any closer.

There are actually TWO reasons for the fatigue.

One is poor health due to poor eating habits, poor sleep habits and poor physical conditioning. Most folks are horribly out of shape and do not have the energy, stamina or endurance to drive to the fruition of their dreams because their bodies cannot handle it. I am not going to get started on that subject here, but according to Dr. Daniel G. Amen, M.D. (doctor of adult psychiatry and neurology) at Amen Clinics (www.amenclinics.com), poor eating habits and the climb of obesity in America has resulted in a continual decline in decision making, thinking and problem solving abilities. This is totally a little voice issue that simply requires commitment, discipline, and good coaching to solve.

Yet even if your body is in reasonable health, you may still be too fatigued.

Why does this happen and how can you fix it? You guessed it—it's all about the "little voice." If I could use Alan Walter's example for a moment, he describes us all as having come into this world with an abundance of "Life Force Particles."

Alan says:

> *The basic force in the universe is life-force; particles are small pieces, bits, fragments or parts of a whole. Life-force particles then can be defined as fragments of the life-force known as YOU. Therefore your power and energy*

levels (moods) are determined by the quantity of life-force particles you have available.

He goes on to talk about:

How Life-Force Particles are Trapped and Lost

Example: Imagine this is the flow of the river of your life. Let us hypothesize that you came into this life with two-million positive life-force particles available.

2,000,000	Prenatal	
−269,500	Birth	Your birth was traumatic.
	Age 2	
	Age 3	
−117,500	Age 4	You have many childhood sicknesses.
−31,400	Age 5	First day of school: you are laughed at by the other kids because of your funny name and physique.
−48,800	Age 6	Your parents move; you lose all your friends.

See what I mean?

−74,000	Age 15	You get caught stealing money.
−78,500	Age 16	You get cut from High school basketball team crushing your dreams of being a basketball star.
−69,000	Age 18	You fail algebra.
−397,400	Age 21	Broken love affair; a major paradigm crash.
−170,200	Age 23	Applying for a job, you are turned down by numerous companies before one hires you. You end up in a job you didn't really want.

Footnote 1. These excerpts and the complete explanation of Life Force Particles can be found in Alan's book *The Secrets to Increasing Your Power, Wealth and Happiness*, Wisdom Publishing Company at www.knowledgism.com.

You lose money, your first business venture fails, and ... I think you're getting the picture.

So by the time you are in your 30s, 40s or 50s your energy is so low so you just may have a harder time cranking it up. Your little voice is telling you that you should be slowing down at this stage of your life rather than speeding up. The problem is that even though you are smarter, more experienced and a bit more savvy, you don't have the energy, being-ness, push or presence to drive a big mission across the line. In a word, you are too old! And by old, I definitely do not mean in chronological age—simply in energy. I see it all the time. Great people, with great visions and great ideas, but already on their down-hill slide.

Of course, this doesn't have to be the case. The thousands of examples of great accomplishments by those beyond the middle-age of their lives abound. Harlan Sanders of KFC, Thomas Edison, and so forth.

SO what is the solution? Learning and understanding the processes that are designed to recuperate those lost and dispersed Life Force Particles. They are processes that are designed to remove the subconscious frozen and sometimes hidden upsets and shocks from the past and thus heal your spirit and re-build your energy. (For more on these processes go to: www.knowledgism.com)

It is these processes that I have continued to learn and be coached on for so many years. It is these processes and techniques that have allowed myself and others to continually expand our games, increase our reach, deepen our relationships and improve our health to the degree of being in better shape than most people half my age.

This restoration of dispersed Life Force Particles is critical for all of us, but particularly critical for women on a daily basis.

A good friend of mine by the name of John Gray, who wrote *Men are from Mars, Women are from Venus*, observed that women throughout human history have taken on the multiple roles of caring for the children, maintaining the household, handling the finances, supporting the community, facilitating the education, while men primarily have operated in single-mission-focused manners such as hunting, fighting, waging war, building, etc.

As a result, John says, women are predisposed to "do so much for so many others." The problem is that in doing so, they are continually giving their energy, attention, care, and thus their life force out to everyone—all over the place. And guess what? By the end of the day they are tired and exhausted.

Nearly every husband I know will verify that the number one complaint that his wife has at the end of the day is that she is tired. And the truth is that she is—for GOOD REASON.

But here is the good news. One of the fastest ways for anyone to bring Life Force Particles back is summarized in one word: GRATITUDE. By simply showing, exhibiting or expressing gratitude, you are actually attracting back to you those dispersed particles and energy units.

How do you do it? Alan's process for this is simple. By showing gratitude or appreciation for those things that you personally value in your life on a daily basis, you attract more of what you want and more of who you really are. Family, health, wealth, love, teams, relationships, etc.

Look, it's simple! If you want to attract a punch in the nose, punch someone else first! If you want to attract a hug, hug someone else. If you want more appreciation, love, respect—show some!

Being grateful for what you have and showing appreciation and acknowledgment to others bring those particles back to you and to those around you respectively.

A simple "Thank you" and heart-felt acknowledgment is like pumping new energy, new blood, new life into someone.

Alan taught many of us his daily gratitude exercise that is designed to help you regain that energy and spirit every day. Everyone that I know who has used it consistently for at least week reports mysterious but wonderful meetings, occurrences, resources and opportunities showing up in their lives.

As you regain your life force, you also regain your brilliance and size and you start attracting more and more of what you are grateful for. This is how the rich get richer, the healthy get healthier, and how you can be the big being you are meant to be. Alan says that once you start doing this, you will find yourself in the right places at the right times, with the right people, the right resources, the right answers, and the right results.

#3 is BECAUSE THEY JUST CANNOT WIN!

There are some people, no matter what resources you give them, who cannot hold onto them, cannot sustain success or will find some way to mess up a good thing. Know anyone like that? It's because, as I said in chapter eight, their self-concept is too low. Their self-image sees them as too small, too inexperienced, haven't yet earned the right or whatever. They think that some day when they have more time and money, they will work on their dream. As opposed to BEcoming who you want to BE NOW. Be the great business owner, parent, communicator, friend, or entrepreneur that you strive to be NOW. See, feel and experience yourself as you are now. Change your self-concept.

#4 is QUITTING TOO SOON.

Soooooooo many people quit before they get to the win. I have witnessed countless individuals who gave an idea great effort, but let their little voice take them out of the game. A little voice like, "This is never going to happen, It's taking too long, it's too hard, too difficult, too, whatever." The unfortunate thing is they end up quitting and abandoning their dreams and ideas too soon. The turning point is just around the corner but they don't see it.

Whenever you start something new or when you try to make a change, your competency in that arena will tend to be low. Right? For example, let's say that you want to be in great shape, but your arms turn to Jello after five pushups. Worse yet, after two or three workouts, you are so sore you cannot even move. Or more commonly, you lost a few pounds right up front on your new fitness program, but now the scale isn't moving and you feel like you are getting nowhere.

At the same time, your level of frustration is high. You want results faster. You're sick of being weak. The work is hard. This is normal. Unfortunately it is at that moment when the little voice kicks in and gives you every reason why this is not worth it. "It should not have to be this painful, I'm too old for this, There has to be a better way, My body is not designed for this," and you even find evidence around you to support the abandonment of your process.

Yet over time, if you just stick with it and endure the learning curve, you will get better and there will come a day or a moment when you have that "AHA!" moment. It is that moment when your little voice says, "Wow, I actually feel stronger." "Gee, I literally bounded up those steps." "Someone said I look better."

And with that little win, that little AHA, you feel fueled up to keep working, learning, and growing as you watch your competency grow and your frustration replaced with confidence and pride. The problem is that most QUIT before they get to that AHA moment.

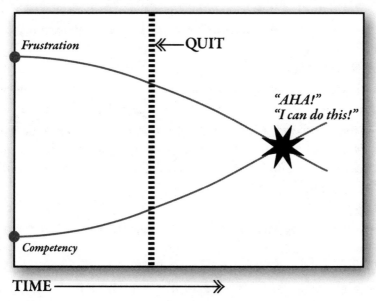

Graph 1. Frustration/Competency Curve
Adapted from Jim Harris, Emotional Learning, *with permission*

What is the little voice mastery solution for this one? You may not like it, but this is my solution. You have to slide that whole curve to the left. In other words, force yourself to the AHA moment before your little voice can talk you into quitting. How? Through applying these components:

I will use the example of getting in shape with my fitness coach Mack Newton:

1. **High frequency** and **focused immersion** into the thing you are looking to master. You study, think and talk about working out and being healthy. It pervades your whole life. You buy into your goal unconditionally. You go to your workouts every day.

2. **High impact experience** of going for it. Each workout is intense and precisely focused

3. **Short duration of time** allowed for that experience to accomplish the task. The workout is 10 minutes of stretching and 35 minutes of hard workout—not 3 hours.

4. **Controlled environment** to ensure accelerated learning, elimination of distraction, tight rules of behavioral conduct and performance. You workout with a trainer in their facility and under their supervision.

5. **High accountability** to numbers and stats and **disciplined and direct mentorship** both from a technical perspective and little voice perspective. You get weighed in every day, keep a daily journal of your food and water intake, follow the prescribed training regimen to the letter and surrender to the discipline and mentorship of your trainer who works on your body and your head.

Let me give you an example. In one of my programs where I actually teach people how to build a multi-million dollar business in 5 days, I literally force people to make money. By setting up the environment and rules to support accelerated activity, focusing them to one specific task of selling a specific set of programs, by giving them a seemingly unreasonably short amount of time to complete the task, and by strictly measuring each activity in the selling process, we have had small groups generate over $55,000 dollars of real sales in less than 10 minutes—over half a million dollars in four days!!

Something happens when this occurs. They actually EXPERIENCE themselves as winners. They reach more than an AHA moment. It's more like an "Oh My Gosh!!" moment, such as "I never knew I could do something like that." All of their preconceived ideas of what was possible for themselves, ideas of length of time to accomplish something, how big of a game they could play are completely re-shuffled. They truly experience the real them. In this particular course, I use the game of business and money to literally force money into their pockets so their little voices and their spirit HAVE to believe they can do it. Particularly when they receive a check at the end of the week for the money they made.

Getting you to BE that person that you want to be NOW—by sliding that curve to the left by compressing the time before your little voice has the chance to take you out, will change your life forever. Why? Because once you experience the true power of you and your spirit, you'll never go back. Your little voice may still attempt to slow you down, but you will always remember your bigness.

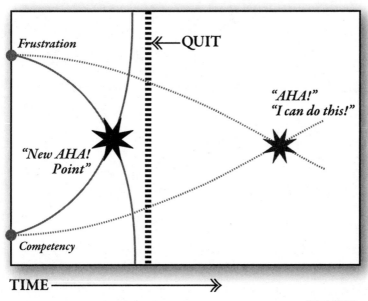

GRAPH 2.
Slide the curve by compressing time before you can quit.

So, to make sure you are not falling prey to failure AND to show your little voice who is REALLY in charge, find which of these four areas may be plaguing you, follow the recommendations and BE the person you want to be NOW!

Our SalesPartners around the world, facilitate a life changing six week, one-on-one Little Voice Mentoring Program that is designed to address most of these issues in about an hour per week. By systematically plucking away at the little voice issues that stand in the way of your income, your dreams and your self-concept, most people earn or accomplish more during six weeks than they do in six months. The power of your spirit is huge. You just need to give it a chance. (For more information on the Little Voice Mentoring Program, and to schedule a 30 minute FREE introductory session, go to www.littlevoicementoring.com.)

Part 2

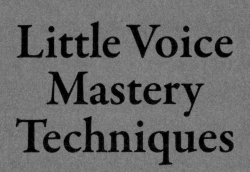

Little Voice
Mastery
Techniques

21 Little Voice Mastery Techniques to Reprogram Your Brain NOW!

Sales is the most important skill to master for several reasons. To increase your income as an entrepreneur, you need to be able to sell to customers in order to generate cash flow, to sell to vendors, investors, team members, lenders, and the public. To be successful in any position in this world, you have to be able to negotiate and communicate for what you want. But sometimes the toughest sale of all is selling you to yourself. Have you ever argued with yourself over a good idea? I thought so.

It's like when you say to yourself, "I need to go to the gym today." Another part of you says, "No, I'm too tired." So then you say to yourself, "Come on you slug— get out of bed!" And your little voice argues, "No. I'm too tired. I went two weeks ago. That's good enough."

Everybody knows that battle. And truly, the secret to making a lot of money and achieving personal success is winning your own internal dialogue. It comes up when you have to raise money, confront your boss, sell to a customer, settle your team, or confront yourself to take action. Every person of wealth knows that battle, and at some level knows how to win it more times than not.

It's self-talk, if you will, that helps them get through difficult, emotional, or depressing times, or times of high pressure. And it's self-talk, or management of the little voice, that helps them turn it around. This is also the same technique that great athletes use. How is it that a guy like Michael Jordan could be sick with pneumonia and still go out on the court and score thirty-plus points to help his team win? What does he do to turn his head around so quickly, so that not only does he change his mind, but he actually changes his own physical prowess?

I have isolated a series of techniques that you can use at any time. Many of these were taught to me by my mentors and coaches over the years. They're called *little voice mastery techniques.*

Earlier, we discussed what the little voice is and who owns it. We covered the fact that it comes from your subconscious memory of certain experiences. And what we know about the subconscious is that it tends to remember those experiences that have emotions attached to them more strongly than others. If there is a negative emotion attached, we might hang on to it a little longer. So, for example, think of the last time you were heartbroken, the last time you lost money, or the last time you loaned money to somebody who didn't pay you back.

I used this example early on in the book, so let's go back to it. Let's say that you and I have been working together for several months. We have a great relationship. Then out of the blue, I approach you and say, "I'm a little short on cash. If you could lend me some money, I'd be happy to pay you back in a month or two." If you have been burned in the past, what happens? Immediately, the little voice in your brain responds with, "Yeah, right! The last person who said that stiffed me. No way!"

Immediately, our relationship changes. You don't trust me quite so much. You keep your distance from me, and you feel awkward when you're around me; yet ironically, it has nothing to do with me. It's about something from your past.

At the very least, you'll be hesitant to loan me the money, and less likely to take the financial risk, for sure. Maybe that's good (especially if I'm not trustworthy). But maybe that's not good because becoming too averse to risk may prevent you from investing in real estate, building a business, or taking necessary steps in order to develop yourself personally or professionally.

That's why these techniques are so critical. They're meant to help you know when and how to override the little voices that hold you back, so that your dreams don't pass you by.

Years ago when I had my first job in sales, I almost got fired because the little voice in my brain was driving me crazy. I had to make cold calls. I had six weeks to sell $10,000 worth of desktop calculators before I could go to sales training, where I would learn to sell computers. I would get in my car and drive around from 9:00 a.m. to about 9:45 a.m., all the while listening to my little voice saying, "They're too expensive! People are going to think I'm an idiot. They're going to think I'm a pest."

As a result, I ended up driving around in circles for an hour or so while I talked myself out of it, and then I'd take a coffee break, which lasted until about 11:00, while I continued trying to work up the courage to go out and talk to somebody. And just when I thought I might get up and try it, the little voice would start in again. "Oh, they'll think it's too expensive," it said. "I can't talk to them. I don't have an appointment. They probably left for lunch already, anyway. And what if they think I'm an idiot?" Then I'd take an early lunch.

I was losing the battle for my own brain! The little voice was beating me up, and I wasn't making *any* sales. Two weeks into this ordeal, my sales manager called me into his office and closed the door. He said, "Singer, you realize that you only have six weeks to sell these things, right?"

I nodded my head. "Okay, good," he said, "because we've been watching you, and we've decided that in your case, we're making an exception."

"Great," I thought. "They see that I really am management material!"

Instead, he looked me square in the eye and said, "So here's the deal. If you don't sell something in the next forty-eight hours, you're fired."

It wasn't what I was expecting or hoping to hear. At that point, I had to do something. I had to override the fear and loathing from my little voice and *make cold calls*. More importantly than that, I had to save my job. At some level, I knew that I had to overcome this hurdle in order to get on with my life. The following day, I made sixty-eight cold calls. I sold nothing. But the good news was that I had reprogrammed the little voice in my brain to stop caring what others thought about me, to be spontaneous, to make it a game, to be resourceful, and to become resilient, nimble, and strong. While I sold no calculators that day, *I had sold me to me*, which for me was the biggest sale of all. The day after that, I made two sales and saved my job; eighteen months later, I was number one in sales.

I don't necessarily recommend that strategy, but I quickly went from being almost fired to becoming number one in sales nationwide, and I've built several businesses since then. I've worked with organizations all around the world helping people make behavioral changes, increase sales, and increase productivity. I've helped turn managers into leaders, I've helped make entrepreneurs rich, and I've helped build championship teams.

The bottom line in all this is that you can learn every clever technique in the book for investing, building a business, selling, and getting your life together, but if your little voice is still beating you up, all those tricks are absolutely useless. Thousands of people sign up for "get rich" programs or programs about investing in real estate, yet less than 5 percent of those people ever make that money. Did you ever wonder why? It's because there are so many little voices talking them out of it!

Think about it: the wealthiest people in the world, including Bill Gates, Michael Dell, or Warren Buffett, are all business owners. Not only that, their number one skill is that they can sell. I'm convinced that Bill Gates had sweat rolling down his back when he first sold Windows to IBM. *It wasn't even his program and he sold it!* Don't you think he was scared? Don't you think his little voice was second-guessing him? Of course. But he had technique, strength, and conviction that got him past that hurdle. The biggest reason people *don't* get what they want is fear.

The reason you have to learn how to manage your little voice is because it's the best way to overcome fear. So in this chapter I'm going to give you the best of the little voice mastery techniques that I have learned over the years from my best teachers, masters, mentors, coaches, and gurus. And yes, there are a few home-grown ones in there, too. Discovering these techniques cost me millions of dollars and a ton of heartaches. I pass these on to you now in the hope that when you are faced with those moments in your life that cause you to feel fear, when hesitation blocks you or when confusion sets in, you will have in your arsenal the techniques, routines, and systems to win the battle for your own brain.

By the way, you do have more than one little voice. That doesn't mean that you're schizophrenic. It means that inside, you have a winner and a loser, a hero and a coward. You have to choose which part of you should come through at which times. If you're feeling depressed, you probably shouldn't be making sales calls or entering into complicated relationship discussions. Does that mean you shouldn't make the call or get involved? No, it simply means you have to pull one of these techniques out of this tool box that I'm about to give you so that you can turn your brain around. That's what these tools are designed for—to turn your brain, your mood, your energy, and your emotions around in thirty seconds or less.

Any single one will do, depending on the situation. These are not necessarily in order of importance or the order in which I think you should learn them. Simply start with the one that resonates with you the most. Or go to www.littlevoicemastery.com/diagnostic and take the free Little Voice Diagnostic Quiz. It will tell you which of these you are strong in and which you need work on. Once you find out, *__practice them over and over again__*. Repetition of the technique is 90 percent of the process.

TECHNIQUE #1
Handling Success
For more insight into techniques 1 and 2, check out Martin Seligman's ground-breaking work in his book Learned Optimism.

What do you say to yourself when something good happens to you? It's great when everybody pats you on the back. You feel like a legend. But often there's that nagging little voice that tells you that it's no big deal, that you were just lucky, or maybe that the accolades are not really meant for you because you didn't really deserve them. You may even feel embarrassed and try to hide from praise.

Martin Seligman did a lot of studies on this kind of behavior. This psychologist studied the behaviors, results, and "little voices" of thousands of salespeople, professional athletes, leaders, parents, and children. Without going into too much detail about his study, let's just say that he found that how you handle success is as important as how you handle failure.

Once you have a success or a win, here's what you do:

First of all, make a fist with your right hand, physically pull it in and emphatically say "Yes!" So far, it's easy, right? I know it seems hokey and you feel stupid, but you need a physical and verbal gesture to *anchor this win into your body.* The reason will become clear later because you will need these techniques to change your state of mind when you are later faced with intimidation. You need to have this technique in place first.

So, with every win and every success you achieve, anchor it in by making a fist and saying "Yes!" Do it a couple of times to emphasize the point. Or, if there is someone else around, give that person a high-five, a handshake: something physical (I don't recommend headbutts). *It is imperative that you do this.*

Now that you've mastered the physical part of celebrating wins, the second technique in this category is aimed solely at the little voice. When in fact you get a win, what does your little voice say about it? Does it say that you were lucky, or does it say that you earned it? Studies show that if you tell yourself, "I deserve this because I've earned it" or "I deserve this because I was prepared," your energy and resilience will increase.

Seligman also found that this approach tended to actually help people create more wins. Even if you win the lottery, don't ever say that it was luck. Instead, say, "I was in the right mindset. I deserved it. The universe is looking upon me kindly now." In other words, take ownership of success. Even though there may be other people to whom you could attribute your success, you need to take personal credit for it as well. The old rule of sales is, if something good happens within a twenty-mile radius, take credit for it! It's only a game you're playing with the little voice in your brain. It will increase your energy. It's not about being delusional; it's about manipulating your own mind into becoming successful.

The third part of this technique is to *tell yourself that the rest of your week is now going to be great.* Have you ever reached into your pocket and pulled out a $20 bill that you had forgotten you put there? From then on, your day starts going great. People start opening doors for you. All the traffic lights turn green for you. Think about it in those terms. Don't think about it in the same terms your little voice might, and say to yourself, "Well, it's a win, but I still have all these other problems." If your little voice starts throwing those little darts, tell it to "Stop!" When you hear it going in the wrong direction, you say "Stop!" Say it out loud if you need to. I know it sounds crazy, *but you have to disrupt and reverse that normal pattern.* You see, you've been told so many times in the past not to "take credit" for things, not to be "too bold." Those comments were designed to keep you small and under control. When it comes to success, own it.

The fourth part of the success technique is to let it just cascade into the rest of your life. You need to tell yourself, "The whole week is going to be great, and because of this I'll bet work is going to be awesome today. My golf game will probably even get better!" If you find the $20 bill in your pocket, you say, "You know, this is a statement of my life. My marriage is great. My business is great. This is a sign from the cosmos that things are going to continue to be great."

Now, I know it sounds ridiculous, but when you think about it, this is what great athletes do. They take the smallest of wins and make them great. How many times have you seen a football game where a team is struggling to come from behind? Each time they gain a few yards, they celebrate. They jump up and down, high-fiving each other and laughing. Why? Because it builds energy, hope, and confidence. They know they have to build that energy in order to carry themselves on to success.

TECHNIQUE #2
How to Deal with Adversity

What do you do when somebody says no to you? It's exactly the opposite of dealing with success. If somebody were to say, "Look, we really like you, but we don't like your product. Don't come around here again," you walk away feeling defeated. This can happen.

What you say to yourself in the first minute or so is very critical. So the little voice mastery technique for that one is the exact opposite of what you do to deal with success.

Don't attribute the problem to yourself personally.

I'm not saying you're not going to take it personally, because that's hard not to do. But what's easier to do is to say, "Obviously, I was not aware of the other circumstances or other products that they were looking at so, while I'm responsible, it's not all because of me."

The thing you *don't* want to say to yourself is, "There's something wrong with me," or "I'm not cut out for this. I knew this wasn't going to work." If you hear yourself saying those things, say "Stop!" enough times that you stop seeing it that way. Look, it doesn't even matter if it's true. You have to learn to control your own little voice. So you attribute it to outside sources.

Secondly, when faced with adversity, say to yourself, "This is an isolated incident, which has no effect on the rest of the week," as opposed to, "The rest of my day is ruined. The whole week is going to be like this." You've got to turn that around and isolate the incident. Do not allow it to become protracted beyond that moment. Even say to yourself, "I've got a new call to make. This is a new page. It's over and done with."

When you are first practicing these techniques, say them out loud. They will have more impact. Some people may think you're crazy, but that's okay. If you watch athletes, many times just before their competitions, you can see their lips moving. High jumpers at the Olympics do this all the time. They're talking to themselves before they go over that bar. They're applying little voice mastery tools of their own to get themselves over that bar. Once you've developed the skills, the rest is in your head. You know what I'm talking about.

And third, *never allow to the problem to be global.* In other words, don't say things to yourself like, "The same thing's happening to me at work. The same thing's happening to me at home and with my friends, and this is also why I'm broke." If your little voice starts saying that, you have to say, "Stop!" Say that immediately and turn it around. Again, isolate the incident. Say something like, "Obviously I had a tough time with this call, but I still have great relationships. This doesn't happen all the time."

We've all felt that "poor me" thing, wondering why these kinds of things *always* happen to us. The truth is, they don't. Think about it. Look at your track record. The truth is that the number of times it actually happens to you is very small compared to the number of incidences. Somebody backs into your car and you immediately think, "Why does this always have to happen to me?" It *doesn't* always happen to you. It happens to you once every five years or so. If it were happening to you all the time, it would be happening five times a day.

So you have to manage your little voice carefully because it can lie to you.

So, after you say, "Stop!" you isolate the incident. Then stack the evidence in your favor and say to yourself, "This *doesn't* happen to me in any other part of my life; it's very isolated. It's not an indication of anything else except that this was a bad experience." Say it out loud, even if you don't believe it. It's a reprogramming issue.

TECHNIQUE #3
How to React in the Face of Fear
Adapted from everybody!!!

Remember when we talked about anchoring success? I gave you a few techniques for how to handle success. Now I'm going to show you how to do that when you're facing something intimidating that creates fear—those things that tie your stomach in knots and send sweat rolling down your back—so that when you find yourself faced with that kind of fear, you won't fall apart into a debilitated heap.

Whether it's making a sales call, talking to your boss, talking to your husband or wife about something that's potentially a touchy subject, asking for money, or even asking somebody out on a date, we've all faced seriously intimidating situations. And no matter the situation, this technique can help.

Let's say the love of your life is sitting across the room. Your heart is beating a hundred miles an hour and you're saying to yourself, "I don't want to look like an idiot. I don't want to get shot down." And if that's what you're thinking on the way over there, guess what? You're going to get shot down. Your brain will disengage from your tongue, as usual, and you'll come across like a dope. So here's what you do: Make that fist, like I told you to do before, remember the last success that you had, pull it in and emphatically say, "Yes!"

Your body is a like a computer—it remembers. When you repeatedly say "Yes!" after every win, your body anchors, or remembers, the success. So when something goes wrong and you say "Yes!" again, your body thinks it's repeating a success and the energy comes back again. It's actually a very Pavlovian response! Your energy will come back up, you'll be more resourceful, and now you can go and introduce yourself to that other person. (By the way, I wouldn't do this in front of the person you are trying to impress. It might just backfire on you.) You're going to be in a much more positive state of mind than before, and you'll reach a much higher level of success.

If I were to isolate which technique is the most important, this one on handling intimidation or fear would probably be it.

TECHNIQUE #4
How to Debrief and Leverage Any Situation

Let's say you have a win. Or maybe you have a failure. Let's say you're confused or in a quandary. After any experience that leaves any sort of an emotional wake, whether it's positive or negative, it's important to know you can move on, because otherwise your little voice stays in a questioning state and you won't grow. It will ask, "Could I have done better? What should I have done better?" Everybody is familiar with this line of questioning, and you need to get rid of it because that takes your energy down. Confusion, or second-guessing yourself, is a very emotionally draining place to be. So here's how you manage this one.

What you do is ask yourself a series of very simple questions after any emotional situation:

1. **What happened?** When you ask yourself this, you can break it down into two parts:

- What worked?

- What didn't work?

For example, you made a sales call and it didn't go well. The following conversation would then take place in your head:

What happened?

"The prospective customer showed little or no interest."

What worked?

"Well, we assessed their needs pretty well, and they acknowledged that. We also were able to build some good rapport, which they also acknowledged."

So what didn't work?

"It seemed that when we started talking about price, they went blank, and when we started talking about implementation they found other things to do, and their eyes kind of glazed over."

Now that you're clear about what happened, you ask yourself:

2. **Why?** Once you start to think about it, your answer may be:

"Well, we didn't do our research.
We didn't have our numbers together."

3. **What did I learn?** Here, you're looking for a pattern of behavior. You might say the following to yourself:
"What I learned from this is that I need to be more prepared to handle issues of price. I need to have a better presentation about price. Instead of thinking about costs, maybe we should call it an investment and focus on value. Instead of talking about how much they're going to have to spend, maybe we should talk about what their ROI is going to be if that's important to them."

4. **What did I learn about me?** Here, your response might be:
"I learned that when I start talking about price, I start getting sweaty, and I know it happens a lot. Maybe I need to get beyond that hurdle and practice objections about price."

Whatever that issue is, you have to address it. And when you ask, "What did you learn?" the issue is no longer one of being right or wrong. It removes the issue as to whether or not you screwed up. You either got the deal or you didn't get the deal, but either way, you learn something.

There are some days when I'm having a tough time, and I have to keep asking myself, "What's the lesson here? What did I learn?" That's a little voice mastery tool that has bailed me out hundreds of times, because sooner or later your brain will say something like:

"You learned that you're an idiot."

That's when you need to respond with, "No. I'm not going to take that one on." Or it might say, "I learned that I should have stayed in bed today."

And you'll need to say, "Nope. Try again," until you get to the real lesson, which is, "I learned that I have to practice a few more presentations in order to come across more professionally."

> *No matter how small the success may seem, celebrate all your wins. Celebrate the wins of everybody around you as well.*

You'll need to keep asking yourself, "What did I learn?" so that you can make significant corrections after that. Don't allow your first reaction or your first little voice response to be the final one. That's called debriefing.

TECHNIQUE #5
Celebrate All Wins!

Remember to anchor success into your body, whether it's with a high-five, a clenched fist, or some other method you prefer. No matter how small the success may seem, *celebrate all your wins.* Celebrate the wins of everybody around you as well. This helps you become accustomed to being a winner and to recognizing that feeling and associating it with yourself. It becomes contagious to those around you. Celebrating the wins of others is also an excellent form of acknowledgment and it helps to remove any resentment you may have toward others, or that they may have toward you. It creates the feeling that everyone is constantly winning. So when you see a win, celebrate it even if the other person is a bit shy about it. They need to learn to own it, too.

TECHNIQUE #6
How to Shift Your Mood Quickly (Slump Management)
Courtesy of Alan Walter at www.knowledgism.com

Sometimes you're in a bad mood. Sometimes you go into a slump. We've all been there. But we can't always indulge our moods, as much as we may want to. The rest of your team, family, customers, or colleagues don't really care that you're having a bad day. Others depend on you, and besides, when you're in a slump, it seems everything just serves to make you more depressed, so there's very little upside to staying there. So here's what you do, and it's very simple.

You play the counselor and the "counselee," and all questions and answers should be phrased as if you were playing these roles. Ask yourself, or someone who needs it, these questions:

Counselor: What mood are you in?

Counselee: Well, I'm depressed.

Counselor: Good, thank you. Now, again, what mood are you in?

Counselee: Actually, I'm a little confused.

Counselor: Thank you. Again please, what mood are you in?

Counselee: Well, I'm not sure what mood I'm in.

Counselor: Let's try again—what mood are you in?

Counselee: I'm frustrated.

Counselor: Think about that. What mood are you in?

Counselee: I think I'm frustrated.

Counselor: Okay.

You don't stop asking the question until you've isolated one mood, and meanwhile, the intensity of the feeling and the energy associated with it will drop. Asking this enough times will actually help the feeling to dissipate. That's how you know it's okay to proceed with the next line of questioning, which is:

Counselor: What game are you playing?

Counselee: Well, I'm playing the sales game.

Counselor: Thank you. What game are you playing?

Counselee: Well, I'm playing a business game.

Counselor: Thank you. Again, please—what game are you playing?

Counselee: I'm playing a game that helps people get what they want.

Counselor: Thank you. What game are you playing?

Counselee: I'm playing the game of serving others.

Counselor: Think about that. What game are you playing?

Counselee: I'm playing the game of serving others.

Notice that the game is now much bigger than just a sales game. That's how you know you are finished with this question. Repeat the question until you're sure it's solid, even if it seems a little annoying. Annoying is good because that's how you know it's time to move on to the next question:

Counselor: How big are you?

Counselee: Well, I don't feel so big right now.

Counselor: Good. Thank you. How big are you?

Counselee: I don't know.

Counselor: Thank you. Again, please—how big are you?

Counselee: *As big as my body.*

Counselor: How big are you?

Counselee: *Well, as big as this room.*

Counselor: Good ... how big are you?

Counselee: *I'm pretty big.*

Counselor: Thank you. How big are you?

Counselee: *As big as the planet!*

Counselor: Think about it. How big are you?

Counselee: *I'm huge!*

Counselor: Good job. Thank you.

The process is now over. But by simply reading this, you've probably found that your body and emotions have shifted a bit. This is a very powerful exercise to try when you're either coaching or being coached by someone else. You can do this with yourself, with your kids, or with your spouse.

It's not about manipulating people. Just explain that this is one of your tools for little voice mastery. Your spirit naturally wants to be big, and this process unleashes that.

I did this with a woman I was coaching who was having some problems with her business. She'd been in a slump for months. I asked her these simple questions, and it only took forty-five seconds to turn things around. In just forty-five seconds, she was laughing

When you make a mistake—celebrate!

and saying, "This is incredible! I can't believe how my mind h₂ such a short period of time!"

Again, there are reasons behind it, but I'm not here to tell yc I don't even know all of them. But it works, and it's a great mood quickly

TECHNIQUE #7
How to Overcome the Fear of Making Mistakes
Adapted from Joseph McClendon III, co-author of **Unlimited Power: A Black Choice** *with Anthony Robbins*

I'll call this stage fright, because anybody who presents, and anybody in sales, will know that unless you get a little knot in the pit of your stomach before a presentation, you're just not normal. I still get it after all these years, and I think everybody does. But I have an interesting way to deal with this. Even Barbara Streisand, who would get nauseated from her stage fright, or world-class tennis players who get the butterflies, use this method.

It's called *celebrating mistakes*. I know it sounds silly, but it's a total reprogramming or rewiring of your brain. We've talked about making a fist and saying "Yes!" to celebrate all wins. Well, you make this one *bigger* because we're talking about a bigger issue internally. So, take both hands, thrust them in the air, and shout, "Yeah!" to celebrate. It's simple—just put yourself in a quiet place, thrust your arms out, and yell, "Yeah!"

Pretend it's a win and celebrate. Do it a few times, but don't forget the arm movement. That part is important.

So when you make a mistake—celebrate! For instance, think about going on stage. The minute that knot forms in your stomach, stop thinking about it and just celebrate! The minute I get nervous, I shout, "Yeah!" and throw my arms in the air. I know it sounds a bit Looney Tunes, but if you repeat it enough times—and it only takes about thirty seconds—you're wiring your brain to celebrate whenever you get nervous.

Think about the repercussions of that. It means that you're learning to love taking risks. The same thing applies once you get off the stage and you start beating yourself up internally for not having given a better performance or presentation. I used to have a tendency to focus on the one thing that didn't work or could have been better. Do you do that? Have you ever come out of a sales call thinking, "I should've, I would've, I could've?" You can deal with that fully when you debrief, but before you get to that point, celebrate. As soon as your little voice starts in with, "I should've ...," you thrust those hands in the air and say, "Yeah!" Just like that.

And when you come out of that sales call or finish the presentation, you find the one thing that *did* work and celebrate that win. Anchor it, like we've discussed, five or six times, and then go into your debrief. Your mindset will be totally different. Your energy and the resourcefulness will rebound through the roof.

Martin Seligman found in the course of his studies that just by making slight changes like this, sales staff results went from 34 percent to as high as 90 percent, just by using such little voice mastery tools.

Celebrate nervousness. Celebrate wins. Even celebrate mistakes. You're going to find that you're 100 percent present, with 100 percent high energy.

TECHNIQUE #8
How to Successfully Deal with Failed or Unaccomplished Goals
Inspired by Allen Wright

I'm going to spend a little bit longer on this one because this is a technique that very few people know about. I call this the "failed goal" technique.

Let's say you want to achieve a certain amount of revenue in sales this year, and let's say you want to generate $100,000 for yourself. You've set the goal. And at the end of the year, although you've been pushing really hard, you still only end up with $90,000. The $100,000 goal that you set for yourself becomes a failed goal. How do you handle that?

You've got to handle it, because if you don't, there can be some very bad consequences. Here's what I mean. You climb along toward this goal and when you don't get it, your energy drops. Then you try to set another goal, but you're now setting this new goal with lower energy. The new goal becomes a little harder to achieve, and maybe you don't achieve that one either. Your energy drops again. After a few of these, maybe you start lowering your expectations of yourself (not good). Ultimately, you stop setting goals completely. You become disillusioned.

I find that many people don't set goals because they're afraid they won't achieve them.

In your lifetime, you're not going to achieve all of the goals you set.

That's a fact. And it's okay. You just need to know how to handle it when it comes up so that you can move on and keep your energy up. Here's my secret little voice mastery technique for this one.

Once it becomes clear that you have not achieved the goal, sit down and make a list. I recommend that you do this in writing. If you choose to do this by talking it out, at least record it, because you'll be amazed later on by what you hear yourself saying that you didn't realize you were saying at the time.

Reiterate the goal. What things *did* you accomplish on the way to that goal? Write them down. So you didn't get $100,000, but let's see what you did get. You opened up a new market. You learned a lot about your competition. You actually got a promotion in the process. You were able to buy a new car. Your family is very proud of you. See what I mean? This exercise is even more useful if you do it with someone else.

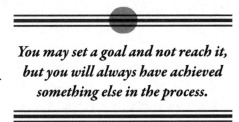

You may set a goal and not reach it, but you will always have achieved something else in the process.

Now, read what you've written or play back your recording and listen to yourself. Which one fills you with the most positive energy? Which one makes you light up? If you're coaching somebody else on this, watch the eyes. At what point does he or she light up?

Pay attention to the times when your passion and energy increase. Chances are, you achieved a different goal that you didn't even know you had. Maybe your secret inner goal was to be recognized by your boss as being a great salesperson, and in the end, you were promoted and your spirit became happy. Maybe that recognition was all your spirit really wanted, and now it's waiting for you to set a new goal. That $100,000 was never your real goal. Something else was beneath it.

I've also set sales goals for myself that weren't always achieved. And when I've gone back and taken a good look at what I actually accomplished, I start to laugh. For example, I wanted to build a $5 million-a-year business. So I went out and worked at it, but I didn't make the $5 million in the first year. For a while, I was depressed, but when I looked back, I realized that I had achieved the goal of proving to my father that I could build a business. He had actually said to me, "You know, son, I'm really proud of what you've accomplished."

When that happened, you could have taken all the money away because I knew that this was all I'd really wanted. Part of me wanted only to hear that, and I didn't even know it. But when I made that list and saw what was on it, I suddenly realized—Wow! That's what I was really going for!

Your spirit, or the essence of who you are, knows what it wants. Once it's satisfied, it's ready to move on. So set a new goal, something bigger and more meaningful. It doesn't mean you don't have to get the $5 million you originally wanted. It means that now you can set a new, more meaningful goal that automatically includes *at least* the $5 million, and then you can get it.

You have to acknowledge when you attain the unacknowledged goal. That's the key in this process, and it's helpful if you can talk it through with some other people. I've had crowds of 500 people in which I have had them pair off. After five minutes of talking this through and listing all the things they did achieve with their partners, I could see that the energy in the room was growing like crazy. You'd swear you'd walked into a party. People don't even recognize how powerful it is.

When your energy goes up, you can set the next goal, which you may or may not achieve. But your energy will continue to soar, and each goal will get bigger and better, and you will feel better each time. The bottom line?

There's no such thing as not achieving your goal.

You may set a goal and not reach it, but *you will always have achieved something else in the process.* And I believe *that's* why you didn't reach your original goal—because you've already achieved or gained something else along the way. I find that it's usually some sort of recognition or acknowledgment that's been gained. A lot of times that's the real goal behind the monetary one.

TECHNIQUE #9
Achieving Your Goals
In collaboration with Jayne Johnson and inspired by James Halcomb

All of us know that we should set goals in both business and in life, but many of us set them and don't achieve them. Actually, most people don't even set them. So here's another little voice mastery technique that will *help increase the probability of achieving your goals.*

When you sit down to write out your goals, whether they're personal or professional, remember they must be measurable and they must be assigned to a specific time frame. Then share them with somebody else and have that person read your goals back to you. Notice what your little voice says as you listen. Are your goals clear? Do you get excited about them? Do you need to reword them? Are you ashamed of them? Are you proud of them? Do you think they're overstated or unreasonable? Whatever the case may be, you need to talk it through.

What reactions does your body have to hearing these goals? Does it react positively or negatively? If it's negative, go back and celebrate like I advised earlier. You have to override that negative feeling. Use the little voice mastery technique you already learned for overcoming the intimidation or fear.

I don't know of any entrepreneur, leader, or adventurer who doesn't have fear.

It's a completely natural response. But the issue is whether the fear paralyzes you or motivates you. So if you learn to celebrate the fear, it's not about being crazy, it's about using the fear to become motivated, thereby increasing your energy.

Additional hint: Write your goal on a Post-it note. Then take a large piece of paper (something like 3′ x 4′) and stick your goal on the far right hand side of the page. Now write down each measurable activity that it will take to achieve this goal, one per Post-it note. Arrange these "mini-goals" or milestones in chronological order across the page, left to right, as they take you from present to future. Create a timeline across the bottom and connect all the Post-its with penciled lines to form a plan. You may have several flows of events moving in parallel lines across the paper. This is called multi-tasking, and it's good.

Voila! You now have a visual representation of how you are going to achieve your goal. Put it up on the wall. Make sure the dates are aligned, and celebrate after you achieve each milestone along the way.

This is called a PERT chart. This process will hold you and your team accountable, and it will force you to look in the mirror constantly. Remember, they are Post-It notes and can be moved, rearranged, and added to as need be. A plan needs to be flexible.

Technique #10
How to Be Totally, 100 Percent Present
Courtesy of Jayne Johnson at www.theclearingsight.com

This little voice mastery technique is very powerful. If you have infants, this is really easy to do. It takes two people, or you could do this in a mirror with yourself. Sit knee-to-knee (you don't have to touch each other) and look at each other, eyeball-to-eyeball, without talking. I know it seems weird, but the purpose of this is to get you present and centered when you're feeling scattered, overwhelmed, or frenzied, or if you simply need to be totally focused when approaching a challenge.

The rules, as you face each other, are no talking and no flinching for at least three minutes. If you can do it for longer than that, great. The little voice in your brain will start going crazy. "This is nuts," it will say. "What does this person think of me? I don't want to do this. I've got other things to do."

That's okay. Just let your little voice run on. You don't have to do anything in this one, just do your best to stay in the present. If you can do this, you'll find magical things happen. All of a sudden your brain will become very quiet. You'll be able to listen to yourself. You can connect with the other person. That doesn't mean you have to be in love with that other person. You don't need to find him or her attractive, or even like that person. You just have to remain present.

After a while of practicing this, your ability to connect, listen, and stay in the moment will be incredible. The next time your spouse talks to you, you will *really hear it*. The next time your sales prospect tells you something, you'll feel connected, instead of listening to your little voice on overdrive as it scrambles for answers. You will find people attracted to you because somehow they feel connected, understood, and acknowledged.

If you laugh, it's totally normal. If you flinch, that's normal, too. It's also normal to look away. Don't beat yourself up—just re-focus and keep going until you can do it for at least three minutes without laughing, flinching, or looking away. Plus, laughter helps to release emotions, so it's a great way to relax and become peaceful.

I do this in the mirror sometimes myself, just to get myself back to the present moment. It's more powerful, however, if you can do it with someone else.

TECHNIQUE #11
How to Anchor Love to Give You Power in the Moment
Adapted from Anthony Robbins and Marshal Thurber

One of the most powerful things you can do to keep yourself strong is to anchor love. We talked earlier about anchoring success, but anchoring love is probably even more powerful. Do this when you need courage, strength, and support.

Go back into your past and recall a time when you knew you were 100 percent, unquestioningly loved. This could be a time from your childhood or an adult moment with a spouse or your own child. Just remember as much as you can about that time: what it felt like, what was taking place, and what you said to yourself. Can you recall this?

When you can see it and feel it again, make a fist and just quietly say, "Yes!" This is now a different little voice mastery technique, one that gives you strength in the face of fear.

> *When the stakes are high, I go to a time in my life when I felt completely loved.*

There are two moments that I repeatedly go back to. The first is the day before Eileen and I got married. She looked me in the eye and said, "I'm never, ever going to leave you." It was a truth spoken directly from her heart to mine, and even now, over twenty years later, I remember it like it was seconds ago. And as I write about it, I can still feel the warmth in my chest.

The second moment is the day my son Ben was born. When they brought him out of the delivery room, he was only seconds old. His eyes were wide open and I reached out to touch him. His hand touched mine, and I looked into those bright blue eyes of his and that was it. It was pure love.

I go back to those moments anytime I want. It gives me enough strength to take on anybody in any situation, no matter what. So anchor love as well as success.

This is one of the most powerful little voice mastery techniques. If your little voice just said, "I don't have a time like that," tell it to shut up, because you do. Everyone does. Be diligent and search. You'll find it.

TECHNIQUE #12

How to Use Bragging to Expand Your Presence and Change Your State of Mind
Courtesy of Robert Kiyosaki

I love this one. If you really want to get your energy up, or if you just want to have some fun, I recommend doing this with a bunch of other people, although you can do it by yourself. It's relevant to any situation, whether it's with sales, your tired body, or just a blue funk.

You give yourself just one minute, or if you're really bold, two minutes, to brag about anything. Talk about anything that you've done in a big, bold, and outrageous way. Become a legend in your own mind for at least a minute. Talk as loudly as you can. Stand on tables if you need to. Yell it. Make

Become a legend in your own mind for at least a minute.

huge gestures. Just keep it going for sixty seconds. Even if your brain runs out of things to say, make it up, do what you have to in order to keep it going. Why? Because it's hugely therapeutic.

If you're in sales, you could say things like, "I am the greatest salesperson on earth! People simply cannot refuse me, ever! You know why I'm so good? I have read more books, listened to more tapes, gone to more seminars, and spent more dollars on education to learn how to sell and become more powerful than anybody on the planet, and that's why nobody can touch me! People just melt when they see me coming. Not only that, but I am SO good-looking that they all want to buy from me, just so they can hang out with me ..."

As you can see, it can get a bit delusional. But two great things happen when you do this. First, and most obvious, it increases your energy. Second, it actually starts giving the little voice in your brain the message that you *are* great, that *you can do things*. It also reminds you of the things that you have done well.

By the way, it's not really necessary to tell the truth in this exercise. For the purposes of this technique, it is okay to lie, fabricate, and exaggerate. It's just a game. But ironically, even though you're making some things up, you might actually find that what you thought was fantasy is pretty darn close to the truth.

Some of us may still struggle with this kind of bragging—it just doesn't feel normal. And that's okay. We've all felt that way to some extent. But even if you can rant, rave, and shout about even your minor accomplishments, you can start to feel pretty good about yourself. For example, "Did you know that I made it to work on time today? Do you realize how *great* that is?!" It doesn't have to be anything fantastic.

Your little voice may be saying, "But I haven't done anything great, so what do I have to brag about?" And right then, tell your little voice to "Stop!" and brag about *anything*. What happens is that you begin to break through your inhibitions and release your fear, shyness, and concern about what other people think about you.

The most powerful part of the bragging process is that you can invent it. It's about having fun with it. The power of technique lies in its ability to break you out of your shell and stop you from worrying about others judging you. Any great leader or great businessperson at some point has learned to quit caring about what other people think.

Whether you do this a couple times a week or just once in your lifetime, you'll see a noticeable difference. When you do this with a group—a sales team, a group of co-workers, your family, or your friends—you'll see everyone's energy soar, and you'll all find that your confidence has increased. And ultimately, if all goes well, you'll all be more ready to try new things and proceed toward your goals. Get everyone ranting and raving. Have them be the biggest, loudest egotists on earth, if only for a minute or so.

TECHNIQUE #13
How to Handle Any Objection Under the Sun

In our SalesDogs *Sales Training Kit,* we use flashcards for an exercise on handling objections. This is a little voice mastery technique that uses the simple idea of repetition. You write down your worst nightmare objection on flashcards: things people might say that are hurtful, intimidating, or indelicate, and literally run drills on these objections with a partner. Some of the most feared objections might be, "You don't know what you're talking about," "You're stupid," or "You're ugly."

For this technique, have your partner fire these objections at you verbally. For example, your partner might say, "I think you're stupid." And you would then say, "Thank you. Why do you say that?" Like the counselor/counselee exercise we did in an earlier technique, you simply repeat the drill over and over again until it doesn't fluster you to give an answer. Each time, you'll feel the pressure ease, your emotions will lessen, and your intelligence will increase.

I'd advise doing this exercise knee-to-knee to get the greatest impact out of the exercise. Your partner should be as harsh and difficult as possible on you, and every time you hesitate, get flustered, or become tongue-tied, he or she should say, "Stop!" Then, have him or her repeat the objection. Deal with the same objection over and over, as many times as necessary to get through a response calmly, without emotion, and without stopping. Then do another one. This is a great way to get over your basic fear of looking foolish in front of others.

TECHNIQUE #14:
How to Banish "Should've, Would've, Could've" Thinking and Regain Power

When you're feeling that you've failed to accomplish something, and your little voice starts beating up on you, it's time to make another list. This time, your list will include all the things your little voice says you should have done, could have done, or would have done.

For example, your list might read, "I could have gone to the gym," "I should have called my mother," or "I would have made more sales had I made more calls." List every single thing you can think of. Just be as whiney as you can possibly be.

Then read them carefully, over and over again, considering each one. If you have to, add to the list until you get them all out. Interestingly enough, at some point you'll find them humorous, you'll laugh, your energy will lift, and your guilt will erode as you're able to let each of them go. This magical little tool sort of cleans up and corrects that little voice in your brain.

The cool thing about this technique (and actually, the rest of them, too) is that if you repeat the techniques, they become automatic. You may not even need to write them down, because if you've practiced them enough, your brain stops making those justifications.

As for that pesky guilt, you can try this, although I'll warn you, it's a tough one. When you get to feeling guilty about a failed accomplishment, assume a push-up position on the floor and hold it for as long as you insist on feeling guilty. Stay there until you let go of that guilt, even if your arms are quivering and the sweat is rolling down your forehead. It's not so easy, is it?

Maybe next time, you'll ease up on yourself.

This technique is actually good for anything that your stubborn little voice simply won't let go of.

TECHNIQUE #15
How to Pinpoint Your Real Emotions
So You Can Free Up Your Energy—Every Time
Courtesy of Lawrence West

You can use this powerful technique on yourself, although it's even more powerful if you use it with others. I call this *identifying the emotion*. Sometimes people get emotional and they don't even know that emotion is dictating their actions. While it's not your job to solve someone's problem, this technique will help you to accurately pinpoint the real emotion at work and to receive verification that you're on track. It goes like this:

"I really hate when people like you keep bothering me."

"What is it that you're upset about?"

"I'm not upset!"

"Okay. You seem angry."

"I'm not angry, I'm annoyed."

"Oh, so you're annoyed. What are you annoyed about?"

"I'm annoyed when people like you keep bothering me. It annoys me."

"What annoys you about that?"

"What annoys me is the fact that my time is precious and I have things I have to do. I wouldn't mind talking to you at another appropriate time if ..."

The emotion has been identified and acknowledged, and now the prospect, customer, friend, or partner is able to talk to you about the real problem. Rather than trying to justify your own position or trying to fix something, you instead try to identify the emotion of that person's little voice.

This technique works on both sides of the equation. When you're upset or emotional, you have to ask yourself the questions. The important thing here is that you do your best to identify the emotion, particularly if it's a negative one: "Do I feel angry right now? No, I don't feel angry. Do I feel frustrated? Yes, I feel frustrated." The second you identify what your emotion is, your energy begins to lift again. Without identifying the correct emotion, we tend to blame others, thinking that the problem is our boss, our clients, or our family. That's justification and blame, and it gets us nowhere.

Feeling "upset" could come from confusion, frustration, anger, fear, or even sadness. It could be anything. But your goal in this process is to find out *the emotion you're feeling now.*

Here's a list of emotions to keep with you, just as a reminder:

Enthusiasm

Impatience

Anger

Distrust

Upset

Joy

Hostility

Sadness

Fear

Apathy

Confusion

Needing acknowledgment

Terror

When someone else in your life or your business is clearly in an emotional state, try this. It might sound a little something like this:

"Well, how are you feeling right now?"

"I don't care how I'm feeling."

"Are you angry?"

"No, I'm not angry!"

"Well, you're upset about something."

"I'm sort of upset. I guess I'm just confused."

"Oh, you're confused?"

"Yeah, I'm confused."

Then you'll notice their tonality shifting, and they'll be more calm and thoughtful. You have to talk to that little voice and ask it which emotion is at work because sometimes people can't identify it for themselves. You don't even have to deal with it—just acknowledge it. Then, if you want to deal with it, go ahead. But first, *identify* it.

Don't deal with the issue. Identify the emotion.

Remember that high emotion yields low intelligence. That's why you have to let the emotion dissipate first before you can talk about anything intelligently.

TECHNIQUE #16
How to CHOOSE How You Want to Feel
Adapted from Lynn Grabhorn and her book Excuse Me, Your Life is Waiting

Have you ever been excited about a great idea you've had, and when you shared it with someone else, he or she looked at you, unfazed, and said, "Yeah, so?" You were enthusiastic and the other person was apathetic.

On an emotional scale, they're light years apart. In fact, you'd find "apathy" somewhere close to "dead" on that scale, just below fear, sadness, anger, or frustration. And probably right up top, you'd find "enthusiasm."

So, your job in this technique is to identify where you or someone else falls on the emotional scale, and to help that emotion to rise up the scale accordingly.

For example, I might say to myself, "I'd rather be enthusiastic right now."

And then I'd ask myself, "Well, where am I on the emotional scale?"

"Well," my little voice might say, "I just don't care."

"No, it's not that I don't care. I'm just afraid."

"Is it really fear?"

"No, it's not fear. It's frustration. That's what it is. I'm frustrated."

"So what's the frustration?"

"Well, I can't seem to get the resources I need to get all of these projects completed on time ... "

Once I've identified the emotion I'm really feeling, then I can ask myself, "How do I want to feel right now? Do I want to feel enthusiastic? Do I want to feel depressed?"

If you're doing this with someone else, once you've identified his or her true emotion, ask, "How would you rather feel?" Then you can talk about what it would take to make that happen. By this point, the person's mood will naturally improve and the energy level will increase.

If it's your mood being called into question, ask yourself how you want to feel and then allow yourself to feel it. If you can't make yourself feel it, recall a time in the past when you did feel it, or at least a time that put a smile on your face. By that time, you'll know your energy is coming back up.

One moment I like to recall is when I watched my son kick his first goal into the net in a soccer game. I smile every time I think of him jumping up and down with that big, Cheshire cat-grin plastered on his face. Before I know it, I'm back to where I want to be emotionally.

This is a powerful technique to deal with any emotion—even grief, which is way at the bottom of the scale. It's okay to grieve for a while, but at some point you need to ask, "How long do you want to be sad?"

Your little voice might say, "I'm tired of being sad already."

Then you have to ask yourself, "How do I *want* to feel?"

Then recall a time when you felt the way you want to feel, or recall a time when you were with somebody else who felt that way. What did it look like? How did it feel? If you do that, you'll quickly turn your emotions around.

TECHNIQUE #17
How to Bring Yourself and Your Group into the Present
Adapted from Marshal Thurber

This is a technique for controlling the little voices of an entire group. I call it "What I feel like saying." You actually sit around before any meeting or gathering, and everybody takes a turn at saying, "What I feel like saying is ..."

The key word here is *feel.* And all you're allowed to do is say how you feel. For example: "What I feel like saying is that I'm really tired and I don't want to be at this meeting." Everyone else responds by simply saying, "Thank you."

But here are the rules: Nobody is allowed to chime in, and nobody is allowed to agree or disagree, by saying things like, "Oh, I feel that way too," or "I don't feel that way." You just listen, and when that person's done, you say, "Thank you."

There also must be a time limit on it. Usually, thirty seconds or less is great, but if you have a big group, then five seconds or less per person is appropriate.

How many times have you been in a meeting where several people have mentally checked out? This technique is a way of quieting the little voices that are all over the board and getting everyone back on the same page and in the present. It also allows people to quickly vent their emotions.

And if you're by yourself, and you find your emotions running high as you deal with another person, ask yourself, "What do I *feel* like saying?"

I've been in some sales calls where I was filled with so much emotion that my body was shaking and I didn't know why. Was it nervousness? Anticipation? Something else?

So, I would say to myself, "What I feel like saying is that my body's shaking right now and I'm not sure why."

Then something in my brain will say, "I feel like there's something else here, something that's not on the table," or "I feel nervous about the next sales call I have to make." Once you've laid it on the table, you can move on.

Remember, there are no repercussions and no rebukes to what anyone says. This must be done in a "safe place" that allows you to get back in the moment and on with business.

TECHNIQUE #18
How to "Call It": Clearing Up the Unspoken Problems That Block Success

Whenever your little voice chimes in, you've got to call it—tell it like it is—like this: "It appears that this is going on right now," or "What I think is going on is this." You can use this in a sales call, when you sense that something is going wrong or your little voice perceives a problem. You simply stop, and you call it.

Here's an example: "It seems to me that there are some things going on that aren't kosher, or aboveboard."

Now, if you're wrong, it's no big deal. They'll say, "No, everything's fine." But if there IS something going on, you will have put it on the table and gathered everyone's focus and

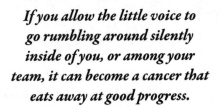

If you allow the little voice to go rumbling around silently inside of you, or among your team, it can become a cancer that eats away at good progress.

attention. Now you have the opportunity to deal with personal agendas or issues that could otherwise undermine the whole conversation. It brings everyone's little voices out into the open.

You also need to call yourself out. It's important to know what's going on in your own head. Acknowledge it and put it on the table, whether it's verbal, on tape, or in writing. Once you call it, you'll find that many of your concerns will start to dissipate.

The point is that if you allow the little voice to go rumbling around silently inside of you, or among your team, it can become a cancer that eats away at good progress.

TECHNIQUE #19
Overcoming "I Can't Do It!"
In collaboration with Jayne Johnson

The little voice can paralyze you if you let it, especially when it says, "I can't do it." It usually happens when you're overwhelmed, depressed, confused, under pressure, or just having one of those days when you want to choke the next person that gives you something to do.

Just remember that it's all in your head. The size of the game that you play reveals the size of your spirit. Never let the little voice get in the way of that game.

"I can't" rarely means that you actually can't. What you're really saying is, "I don't want to" or "I don't know how to" (which we'll handle later). I'm sure you already know this. And parts of this technique work brilliantly when others on your team try saying "I can't" to you.

First, as in all little voice mastery techniques, when you hear it, say, " STOP!" It's best to say it boldly, strongly, and out loud. Try it now ... STOP! Good.

Now that you've stopped the chatter for a moment, you can try one of the following:

1. Say to yourself, "I can't do it," and then embellish or exaggerate. For example, "I can't because it's Tuesday," "I can't because I am wearing a blue shirt," "I can't because my mother-in-law said so," or "I can't because my eyes are blue." You get the picture?

The more ridiculous you make these, the better. Be crazy and spontaneous, and do it as fast as you can. Keep doing it until it gets so silly that you laugh or lighten up about it.

2. Ask yourself this question: "What *can* I do?" Come up with as many things that you can do as possible, and be honest about them. For example: "I can brush my teeth," "I can drink water," "I can tie my shoes," "I can write my name," "I can speak out loud," "I can breathe," "I can walk and talk at the same time," and so forth.

Again, say them out loud and as fast as you can think of them. Eventually, you'll start to feel a bit lighter.

3. Ask yourself, "If I *could* do this thing (whatever it is), what would be the first thing I would do?"

Your brain will answer the question with something very practical and resourceful, helping to get you on track and push through the task at hand.

4. Say to yourself, "It's not that I can't. It's that I don't want to. What is it that I really don't want to do?"

Your brain will answer that question very clearly. Then ask, "Why don't you want to do it?" If your answer is an honest one, then I suggest you dig deeper to find out what the fear or concern is about doing the given task.

Once you get to the real emotional truth, you'll feel more energetic, your resourcefulness will be greater, and you will undoubtedly create a great strategy for completing the task.

> *How you handle success is as important as how you handle failure.*

Find out what's going on inside of you that wants to sabotage your dreams. Sooner or later, you have to stand in your own heat and reprogram the part of you that holds you back.

TECHNIQUE #20
Overcoming "I Don't Know How to Do It"
In collaboration with Jayne Johnson

Many times when faced with new challenges or risks, the little voice finds ways to bail out rather than pushing forward into the heat of a situation. I have found that primarily with the people who want to go into business for themselves, learn how to sell, build teams, invest, or obtain some level of financial, business, or personal mastery. They seem to stop short when they reach the far edge of what's comfortable. For example, perhaps a new franchisee has been really good at communications and building teams, working on the computer, and creating elaborate spreadsheets.

But when faced with owning a business, those skills are only part of what's needed, and the sales ability, the most important component, is outside his or her comfort zone. And no sales equals no income.

Faced with having tried all their currently known skills and strategies, these folks now face an abyss of unknown territory. Once at the boundary of the comfort zone, the little voice may pop up and say, "I don't know how to do it."

I have found in my years of coaching and teaching that even people who are given tools, strategies, and direction take the "easy" way out and say, "I don't know how" once they reach that area of confusion where they've become overwhelmed. And they do this because it usually works. Why? Because throughout most of your life, when you've said those words, people have usually been more than happy to help you. The problem is that makes you a victim of sorts, because you're surrendering your power to someone else. And if their advice fits your existing models and feels comfortable for you to work with, you might apply their advice.

In my experience of working with thousands of people from around the world, I've learned one truth—fewer than 5 percent of them actually apply good advice they've received from someone else. What about the other 95 percent of them? They find that advice to be outside their comfort zones, so they usually blow it off and either look for more "comfortable" advice or convince themselves that they simply can't do the task at hand, that they aren't cut out for it, or that the giver of the advice is wrong and so therefore they're justified in staying exactly where they are in life.

Whew! I'll get off of my soapbox now. But to me, the biggest obstacle to anyone learning anything is that little four-word sentence, "I don't know how." Nine times out of ten, they have either already been shown how to do it, they've been given the tools to figure out how to do it, or they have observed how to do it a thousand times in their observations of others. So instead of "I don't know how," the response should be "I need to learn how," or "What do I need to learn?"

So here's my thinking on how to manage the little voice that insists it doesn't know how:

1. First, as always, say, "STOP!" loudly and firmly.

2. Next, just like in the last technique, lie about why you "don't know how." It doesn't matter what you come up with. The point is to be

outlandish. For example, "I don't know how because my brother lives in Ohio. I don't know how because pianos have benches. I don't know how because my brain is on top of my head. I don't know how because I have a deformed little toe. I don't know how because pink elephants fly!" You get the picture?

Do your lying loudly, boldly, and quickly until you're either laughing about it or you at least lighten up a little. I guarantee it will bring a smile to your face. You may even notice your little voice wanting to resist this process, to actually resist smiling. Just keep going. When you break through that resistance, you will override that little voice that wants to victimize you and keep you helpless. Some people would rather be clueless, confused, and grumpy than have fun and be successful.

Now, ask yourself this question out loud: "What do I know how to do?" Answer this question as honestly and as quickly as you can. As your energy lifts, increase the weight of the things you DO know how to do, one by one. For example, "I know how to eat. I know how to sleep. I know how to breathe. I know how to read. I know how to work out. I know how to pound nails. I know how to create a plan. I know how to write a story," etc. Got it?

As you do this exercise, you may even experience feelings of pride or "being cool," and that's the point. It's about realizing that you really know how to do a lot of things, and by listing them all, there is a part of you deep inside that will begin to feel acknowledged.

Finally, ask yourself this critical and powerful question: "If I DID know what to do, what would be the first step that I would take?" Your brain will come up with a great answer, and soon it's off to the races.

You see, somewhere in your life, you may have bought into the idea that you're not smart enough, quick enough, or as good as someone else. That is all nonsense. In a way, it created a comfort zone that allowed you to justify why you don't have some of the things that you may want in your life—fitness, money, relationships, love, companionship, or anything else.

All around you are great tools, mentors, and treasure troves of information on how to do just about anything. Never tell yourself you don't know how, unless it is with the excitement of wanting to go learn. The "I don't know how" voices are damaging when they're said out of frustration as a way of justifying your position or making an excuse for mediocre results.

You do know how to be successful. Don't ever let something that someone once said to you a long time ago, something detrimental or negative, affect your attitude or ability to create today.

TECHNIQUE #21
Transferring your Relentlessness

On a very hot summer morning in Arizona, I found myself struggling for air as I came to the last three-quarters-of-a-mile mark of my morning run along the Arizona Canal. The little voices in my brain at this point of a run typically are screaming, "Keep pushing! Don't give up!!! You can do it!!" ... even though my body feels like it's dying. Other voices are saying, "Maybe pushing so hard in this heat isn't good for you. Why do you insist on making everything a struggle? Are we into the 'no pain, no gain' mode again?" This is normal internal dialogue for me when I'm running. I always finish hard and am glad I did, but this particular morning I got another insight with about a quarter of a mile to go.

It was this: Somewhere in your life you push unreasonably hard. I will bet that there is something that you do, that you are relentless about and are willing to override all the negative little voice chatter that would distract you from it. It could be working out. It could be keeping a neat and orderly household. It could be meticulousness around work. It could be the raising of your children. It could be practicing your golf swing. I don't know.

But what I do know is this. You have the ability to override the negative dialogue in your brain that distracts you from your pursuits. If you can do it one place, you can do it in another.

I had a friend who was and is a great skier. He also worked out relentlessly and was in great shape. He was truly unreasonable about skiing and fitness. Yet his personal finances were a mess. He was always on the edge of broke, bitter about never having enough money, and in constant anxiety about his financial future.

When I spoke to him about it he said, "I love skiing and working out, but finances are a pain and I can't seem to get disciplined around it."

I asked him, "Isn't it also painful when you're running up a mountain at 8,000 feet, your lungs are bursting, your legs feel like lead, and your heart is about to explode out of your chest?"

He said, "Well ... yeah!"

So I asked, "Then why do you do it?"

"Because it's good for me and it feels great when I'm done!"

The light started to go on. He had convinced himself that money was different. He had continued to avoid dealing with his financial literacy and had wrapped his self-image up in his physical prowess. His thought had always been, "I may not be rich, but at least I'm in shape!" I said to him, "Why not have both?"

I told him that if he applied half of the intensity, discipline, and little voice management that he used for his body to the development of his financial present and future, he would be in awesome shape.

Today he has bought and developed several great properties in northern Nevada and has not only accumulated an impressive array of property assets, but cash flow from those assets that will handle the needs of his family for many years.

What did he do?

- He found the area in his life where he was already relentless.

- He transferred the same habits, focus, and intensity into an area of his life that needed to be developed.

- He stopped lying to himself, saying that the area that had formerly been neglected was not that important.

- He used the same powerful little voice that pushed him up the mountain to push him to financial wealth.

You can do this today!!!!

Be the awesome, outrageous, and brilliant person that, inside, you know you are.

These are all what I call little voice management techniques. Try to use these on a daily basis. Practice them over and over again until they become instinctual. I guarantee you any situation that arises will give you an opportunity to apply one or more of these techniques to turn your brain around in about thirty seconds.

Remember, when two people come together, the person with the highest energy generally wins. The biggest sale of all is selling to the little voice in your brain. And there's no such thing as a "no sale" call. The question is, which part of you is going to win? You, or the little voice? The call is always yours. But now you have the tools.

Make the choice to win.

Final Story on the Power of Little Voice Mastery

Obviously, I would not write this book if little voice mastery had not made a profound difference in my life. It has. And I think it does for most people at some level. I can honestly say that management of my little voice has not only given me a great life, but has even saved my life.

In a session with one of my mentors, Alan Walter, I had the opportunity to observe pivotal transition points in my life. These were points that until my session with Alan, I had not realized were very profound. I began the session with a feeling of frustration at the lack of public relations and exposure for my business. It was as if I was hiding from the public. Alan began to ask me some very pointed questions and had me recall some of my experiences.

I thought that my shyness in public was due to a painful bankruptcy that I had experienced years ago. I felt that I could not go public until I had once again "earned the right." There was shame and embarrassment blocking my way.

173

But Alan, being the wizard that he is, said, "I don't sense that this is the issue holding you back. Was there something that happened earlier?"

I recalled a Friday evening back in 1984, in Ramona, California. I was standing in front of a seminar room leading a portion of a three-day workshop. I was an instructor-in-training, so I was just learning to teach. My mentor at the time had turned the room over to me to conduct a business simulation game, which I had practiced delivering hundreds of times.

At the end of that game/simulation (which I thought I had conducted brilliantly), I was verbally attacked by a fellow named Sandy. He was one of the most successful developers in Southern California at the time. He jumped up in front of the group and claimed that I had no idea what I was talking about. He said I had never seen a million dollars in my life, it was a stupid game, and I was an idiot for playing it.

Now, if you have any fears of public humiliation, just take a deep breath while you read this, because it was incredibly painful. The whole room of 120-plus people used the opportunity to turn on me. They began yelling, threatening me, cursing me. I had lost the room and was being held over the fire to burn.

The worst part is that Sandy was right. I had no idea what I was talking about. At the time, I had no successful business. I spoke of wealth and had none. I spoke of relationships and had none. It was the most humiliating experience of my life.

When I shared this memory with Alan, he pronounced this to be the cause of my current problem. "That's it," he said. "You've been hiding under the radar since then, waiting for the moment when you feel you have 'earned the right' to the attention."

Then he asked me the most powerful little voice mastery question that I have ever heard in my entire life. **"What ability did you gain** at that moment of pain and humiliation?"

"Gain?" I asked, confused. "I gained nothing. I got hammered, squashed, embarrassed, run out of town. It was the most painful moment in my life."

Calmly, he simply repeated the question. "What ability did you gain?"

It took several minutes, during which he kept asking that same question over and over, when all of a sudden the truth hit me like a ton of bricks.

I transitioned from being a salesperson to a business owner.

One thing that horrible moment had made crystal clear to me was that now, I had to own everything. In that moment, in front of all those people, I was stripped naked of all my charm, words, techniques, and schmoozing ability. It was just me, and, for the first time in my life, I had to face the truth about who I was and what I had, or had not, done. I had to own my life, completely.

And it was painful. But in that moment of 100 percent ownership, I became a business owner.

And then like a cascade of "A-ha's," answers and enlightenment, the rest of my life unfolded. I was able to see that some of the most difficult and painful times in my life were also times in which I had gained new abilities. It was as if each of these trials were extreme heat and pressure that helped to turn me into a diamond.

I recalled when, in the young life of our trucking company, we were almost put out of business several times. My little voice had kept urging me to quit, to throw in the towel. But in the heat of each battle, something would always spontaneously arouse our scrappy team to create miracle after miracle, until we eventually turned things around. I realized that in those instances, I made a second transition.

I went from business owner to leader.

We made it a raging success story. Yet a few years later, after turning that company over to new owners, who ultimately stripped the business down and stiffed the vendors, I was forced to put it into bankruptcy. I remember so clearly the day I went to court in Los Angeles and watched the judge stamp that file, then put it in a pile of other failed businesses being processed that day.

I left the courtroom more depressed, embarrassed, humiliated, and upset than I can ever recall being up to that point. I walked a few short blocks to the Santa Monica Pier and shuffled out to the end of it. My little voice was in bad shape. I'll be honest. ... I thought about jumping. I had ruined everything. I was a disgrace.

And then I noticed something. There were sea gulls squawking, the sun was shining, there were kids surfing and playing in the sand, and the palm trees were gentling rustling in the breeze. The world would go on. The world didn't care what was going on in my mind. I was able to wrestle the little voice back from the edge of the pier, and as I stood there, I went through another transition.

With tears rolling down my cheeks, I swore that I would do everything in my power to make sure no one ever would have to get to this point. That I would do everything in my power to make sure that no entrepreneur, business person, or individual would have to look down the barrel of the gun toward failure and defeat. That, on my watch, I would do my best to teach, empower, and inspire all those who really want to win, and help them to know that inside each of them is an incredible winner. I would help them to nurture a spirit that would never die—one that, when armed with the proper tools, insights, and little voice techniques, would win.

That day, I went from being a leader to being a teacher.

In the many years that have passed since then, I have been blessed with great successes, great friends, great partners, and a great family, and I can proudly say the same for my team. And as I look back, I'm convinced it's all because of what Alan said to me: that at each of those painful junctures in life, you gain something. You get closer to being that person you're supposed to be. Resisting who you are is what causes the pain.

I firmly believe that there is a genius and a hero inside of you. I believe that everything that's happened along the way may have put up interference in your journey toward achieving and becoming the best. However, by acknowledging the little voice and using the little voice mastery techniques, you can remove the barriers and allow your spirit to soar once more.

You have the power, you have the strength, and now you have the tools and techniques. Win the battle over your mind and have an extraordinary life.

Go Live!

Resources and References

Referred Books:

Fuller, R. Buckminster • *Critical Path, Intuition, Synergetics and On Education*

Grabhorn, Lynn • *Excuse Me, Your Life is Waiting*

Seligman, Martin • *Learned Optimism*

Pressfield, Steven • *The War of Art*

Hill, Napoleon • *Think and Grow Rich*

Bettger, Frank • *How I Raised Myself from Failure to Success in Sales*

Robbins, Anthony • *Unlimited Power*

Prigogine, Ilya • *Order Out of Chaos, From Being to Becoming: Time and Complexity in the Physical Sciences*

Kiyosaki, Robert • *Rich Dad Poor Dad*

West, Lawrence • *Understanding Life*

Singer, Blair • *SalesDogs, The ABC's of Building a Business Team that Wins*
www.salespartnersworldwide.com   www.blairsinger.com

Mentioned Mentors and Coaches:

Johnson, Jayne • www.theclearingsight.com

Kiyosaki, Robert • www.richdad.com

Newton, Mack • www.macknewton.com

Walter, Alan • www.knowledgism.com

White, Kim • www.kimwhite.org

Unfortunately, many of the best mentors and coaches choose to remain anonymous. They are committed to their life-changing work, but do not want the spotlight on them. Their gifts are priceless. Seek your own coaches and mentors who will help find the best in you.

NOW...

See how well you've learned to
master your own "Little Voice"
by going to:
www.littlevoicemastery.com/diagnostic

... and compare this assessment
with the one
you took when you began this book.

I think you'll be quite pleased with your growth.

Be Awesome!

Thousands of Success Stories
Share One Thing in Common:
BLAIR SINGER

Tens of thousands of people have had "Little Voice" breakthroughs and now enjoy abundant lives personally and professionally. Whether in business, sales, leadership, income, health or family...these success stories all share one thing in common: They worked with Blair Singer live. You can, too.

Join Blair Singer live and experience a breakthrough event like no other. Experience every method, means, strategy and system you will need to win the war of your mind, catapult your income, and reach your full potential.

Blair's seminars are fun and high impact—built upon proven, real-world solutions. You will experience the most advanced, how-to training that will supercharge our life, your income, your career and your business beyond what you ever thought possible.

About the Author

The message is clear. In order to be rich and to succeed in business your number one skill is your ability to communicate, sell and teach others how to sell. Secondly, to build a successful business, you have to know how to build a championship team that can win no matter what. Blair Singer has helped increase the revenues of companies and individuals all over the world through giving them the secrets to implementing those critical components.

If the owner or leader of an organization can sell and instill that spirit of ownership, accountability, and team into the culture of the business, incomes soar. If they cannot, it fails. Blair's work with thousands of individuals and organizations has allowed them to experience unparalleled growth, return on investment, and financial freedom.

Blair is a facilitator of personal and organizational change, a trainer and a dynamic public speaker. His approach is one of high energy, intense and precise personal development and inspiration. His unique ability to get entire groups of people and organizations to change behaviors quickly and achieve peak performance levels, in a very short period of time is due to his high impact approach.

He is the creator of SalesDogs®: a methodology that offers life-changing sales and communication success that has helped thousands increase their income worldwide. It is a unique process that identifies and magnifies the natural strengths of an individual or team and converts them into positive results, personal satisfaction and income.

Blair is the author of two best-selling books: *SalesDogs—You Do Not Have to be an Attack Dog to be Successful in Sales and The ABC's of Building A Business Team That Wins.* Both books are part of the Rich Dad's Advisors series. He co-founded an international training franchise called SalesPartners Worldwide™ that delivers guaranteed success strategies that have helped thousands of individuals and businesses increase their income through building championship teams and sales.

Since 1987 he has worked with tens of thousands of individuals and organizations, ranging from Fortune 500 companies to groups of independent sales agents, direct sellers and small business owners to assist them in achieving extraordinary levels of sales, performance, productivity and cash flow. He is one of Robert Kiyosaki's (author of *Rich Dad Poor Dad*) Rich Dad's Advisors who imparts the three most important skills required for success in business: sales, communication, and the secrets for building championship teams.

Blair was formerly the top salesperson for UNISYS and later a top performer in software sales, automated accounting sales, and airfreight and logistics sales, both corporately and as an entrepreneur/business owner. For the past twenty-seven years, he has conducted thousands of public and private seminars with audiences ranging in size from three to three hundred to over 10,000. His clients typically experience sales and income growth of 34% to 260% in a matter of a few short months. His work spans over 20 countries and across five continents. Overseas, he works extensively in Singapore, Hong Kong, South East Asia, Australia, South Africa, and around the Pacific Rim.

Accomplish & Earn More
in the next 6 Weeks

than you have in the
Past 6 Months

With SalesPartners™ 6 Week "Little Voice" Mastery™ Mentoring Program

"In this program, I squashed the little voice in my head that said I wasn't good in sales and reset my commitment and confidence level. After the first 4 weeks of my program **I generated an additional $300,000 in revenue for my business**, over 6 times my original goal!" *Chris Baran, Fuel for Education*

"In the second week of the program my goal was to lose 14 pounds in weight in 4 remaining weeks. At the end of the program **I lost almost 30 pounds!** My husband and I have bought 3 rental properties and I've negotiated a contract for my business to work on an apprenticeship project with another large firm. So many wins to celebrate!" *Sara McManus, Business Owner and Property Investor*

You will receive weekly one-on-one sessions for 6 weeks taking you through a proven process that will help you:

- Become a bigger, **more powerful** YOU
- Have the confidence and capacity to **set goals** that are most important to you and reflect your true desires
- **Maintain accountability** to your goals and stay focused on what matters most
- **Eliminate procrastination**, limiting beliefs, and other self-sabotaging behaviors that hold you back from earning the income you deserve
- Manage the internal chatter – your "Little Voice" – so that you can **make decisions quickly** and confidently
- Experience the power of a daily gratitude process that will propel you towards your goals and **transform your life** and relationships

Blair Singer, CEO of SalesPartners Worldwide, has personally created a training and certification program around his bestselling book "Little Voice" Mastery so only the most skilled mentors facilitate this program.

Schedule your **FREE 30-minute introductory** "Little Voice" Mastery mentoring session with a Certified **"Little Voice" Mastery** Mentor today.
www.LittleVoiceMentoring.com/book +1 (602) 224-7791

Re-Program Your Brain
in as Little as Five Minutes a Day

Whether you're in your car or on a plane, riding the subway, on a lawnmower in your yard, or doing chores around the house ... you can use those moments to **reprogram your brain so that you ... get everything you want out of life physically, financially and emotionally.**

In this CD set Little Voice Mastery Systems™, which is the practice companion to this book, you will gain Blair's surefire "Little Voice" techniques that are proven to re-program your brain so that it starts working with you—instead of against you.

Once you know how, 30 seconds is all it takes to get back on track!

Transform unproductive downtime into little voice mastery quickly, easily and in a way that delivers the results you want. Break through your fears, by-pass doubts, smash through obstacles and multiply your personal income by listening to the Little Voice Mastery Systems CDs. It will change your life—now!

To get your copy of the Little Voice Mastery Systems CDs go to:

www.littlevoicemastery.com/cd

Coming Soon ...

Little Voice Mastery for Parents

Little Voice Mastery for Teens

Little Voice Mastery for Getting Fit

Little Voice Mastery for Golfers

If you want to be notified in advance of these releases, go to:

www.littlevoicemastery.com/newbook